African Images in Juvenile Literature

To Chinua Achebe, Dennis Brutus, Chinweizu,
and others who courageously speak out

African Images in Juvenile Literature

Commentaries on Neocolonialist Fiction

by YULISA AMADU MADDY *and*
DONNARAE MACCANN

McFarland & Company, Inc., Publishers
Jefferson, North Carolina, and London

Acknowledgments: We wish to extend our thanks to Dr. Fredrick Woodard, the director of the African American World Studies Program at the University of Iowa. His liberating spirit and vigorous leadership help shape a program that brings people together from within and without the diaspora.

We are grateful for permission to reprint two essays originally published in *The Journal of African Children's and Youth Literature (JACYL)* (vol. 6, 1994/1995) and for permission to reprint the interview about picture books that appeared in *The Wilson Library Bulletin* (June, 1995). To Penny Whistle Press we extend appreciation for the right to reprint Dennis Brutus' poem, "Voices of Challenge."

Our family members deserve a special thanks: Abi and Ami (Amadu's wife and daughter) for their patience, support, and skill in typing early drafts; Amadu, Jr. (our youngest "consultant"), for his innocent child-eyes and love of life; and Richard (Donnarae's husband) for his understanding and practical support.

British Library Cataloguing-in-Publication data are available

Library of Congress Cataloguing-in-Publication Data

Maddy, Yulisa Amadu, 1936–
    African images in juvenile literature : commentaries on neocolonialist fiction / by Yulisa Amadu Maddy and Donnarae MacCann.
       p. cm.
    Includes bibliographical references (p.   ) and index.
    ISBN 0-7864-0241-5 (library binding : 55# alk. paper) ∞
    1. Children's literature—History and criticism.   2. Young adult literature—History and criticism.   3. Africans in literature.
4. Blacks in literature.   5. Racism in literature.   6. Africa—In literature.   I. MacCann, Donnarae.   II. Title.
PN1009.5.A47M33   1996
809'.933520396'083—dc20   96-38596
                                                         CIP

Manufactured in the United States of America

McFarland & Company, Inc., Publishers
  Box 611, Jefferson, North Carolina 28640

Table of Contents

Preface

When institutions profess their devotion to diversity, they are obligated to fulfill that ideal in specific, institutional terms. At the University of Iowa, the multicultural ideal is best illustrated in the African American World Studies Program—an interdisciplinary program that has made our own collaboration possible.

One of us (Amadu) came from Sierra Leone to teach "Black Action Theater" and "African American Drama," as well as to stage the premier of his new play: "The Amistad Revolt." And one of us (Donnarae) was already teaching in the AAWS program, centering her attention on children's literature, multicultural education, and black cultural history. As we shared our work with students and with each other, our ideas began to range over an expanding intellectual terrain.

The essays in this book are the result of this sharing and are informed by our joint interest in history. Africa's subjection to colonial incursions produced a record replete with accounts of injustice. Yet the incursions continue in the cultural sphere, even in the education of the young. To study this subject in depth is disheartening but not disabling. It requires on our part an interdisciplinary approach—an exploration into social history as well as a concern for the art of literature.

Literary criticism demands close reading but also a sophisticated view of literary "gate-keeping." In the building of canons, someone chooses, someone's interests are served, and some combination of world-views is presented. "Education," writes Michael W. Apple, "is deeply implicated in the politics of culture. Its curriculum is ... always part of a *selective tradition* and is someone's selection, some group's vision of legitimate knowledge."*

*Michael W. Apple. "The Politics of a National Curriculum." In Transforming Schools. Peter W. Cookson, Jr., and Barbara Schneider, eds. New York: Garland, 1995; p. 345.

1

As we condemn stereotyping in these pages without reservation, we are condemning the prevalent tendency to trivialize racism. We are opposing a force that colonizes the mind, inhibits group freedom, rationalizes exploitation, and generally enfeebles a person's sense of worth as a human being. To counteract such a blight requires no special pleading. Instead, our opposition is integral to our understanding of "white supremacy" as a myth, as a malleable and rectifiable imposition on human life.

Introduction

In the United States, Europe, Africa, and other parts of the world, a non-stop clamor is being made for human rights, children's rights, gender rights, journalistic rights, and the list goes on. In the streets placard-carrying demonstrators chant about "pro-choice," "pro-life," and "green peace." And much of the time, the activists are a mix of races and religions; they come from different classes and backgrounds but are communicating with one voice. They foresee changes in conditions because they are mustering the will to challenge engrained belief systems.

African Images in Juvenile Literature challenges a very old belief system, one that deals with myths and stereotypes that tarnish the image of blacks. It critiques praiseworthy picture books as well as many fictional works that circulate distorted impressions of Africa. It deals largely with novels evidencing a white supremacist bias and the reviews that have supplied these works with exceptional critical support. The books themselves are one part of the problem, but the larger issue concerns the professional network that brings these neocolonialist books into the canon—that showers them with honors and thereby promotes their wide circulation in the English-speaking world. We sound the alarm about these works because although they are products designed for amusement, they are also significant cultural indicators.

Indicators of neocolonialism are perhaps to be expected, given the longevity of theories about "race," or, more accurately, the longevity of *racialized* identities superimposed on people of African origin. We should note at the outset that the term *race* is employed in this book in accordance with popular usage, but it must be understood that "race" exists only as a social construct. That is, it is a flexible and fluid concept that is given meaning only through the social process of *racializing* a relationship or condition. Thus relations between "races" are actually relations that have been defined in racialized terms. As sociologist Stephen Small explains: "Social structures, social ideologies, and attitudes have historically been imbued with 'racial' meaning" (29, 36). As applied to skin color and other phenotypic qualities, "race" is not a meaningful category since the differences *within* any phenotypically similar population is much greater than any differences *between* phenotypically diverse groups. Colonialist motivations of non-blacks have generally been the impulse behind negative associations with appearances.*

White racism as a social organism is so embedded in the mainstream superstructure that it is difficult for Caucasians and blacks to trust what they say to each other.† Freedom from slavery and direct forms of colonization in Africa and the diaspora have not been translated into a system of equality. In these essays we are trying to call attention to the way many Western writers for children promote a damaged image of Africa and the African personality—an image that is not essentially different from the distorted picture presented by their journalistic colleagues. Media coverage typically treats Africa as uncivilized and African people as incapable of managing their own affairs. Books for children instill this idea at the earliest stage of life—the time when it can become deeply embedded in consciousness.

E.S.A. Manteaw comments on this anti–African mindset in the media. In *West Africa* he writes:

> What is most worrying are the consequences of this trend: while new stereotypes and prejudices are formed, old ones are reinforced; good human values of peaceful cohabitation of peoples of all races ... give way to dangerous nationalistic tendencies, as evident in Europe and America today [1191].

Manteaw quotes American scholar Noam Chomsky as he draws a connection between media power and political domination; according to Chomsky, "the Western media determines, selects, shapes, controls, restricts news and information material in order to serve the interests of

---

Colonialism (and by extension neocolonialism) is the domination of one group of people by another group for the sake of the latter's material benefit. It precludes the development of the dominated group.

†*White racism is defined as "the socially organized set of attitudes, ideas, and practices that deny African Americans and other people of color the dignity, opportunities, freedoms, and rewards that [are offered] white Americans." This definition is equally applicable to Africa and its relationship to the Western industrialized world. (See* White Racism: The Basics *by Joe R. Feagin and Hernan Vera. New York and London: Routledge, 1995, p. 6).*

dominant elite groups." By analogy, the "elite groups" represent Western states which dominate, says Manteaw, "almost every sphere of life in this small world of ours" (1191).

Children's literature is in the "selecting" and "shaping" business alongside other media. Educational curricula, writes Michael W. Apple, "is never simply a neutral assemblage of knowledge, somehow appearing in the texts and classrooms of a nation... It is produced out of the cultural, political, and economic conflicts, tensions, and compromises that organize and disorganize a society" (345). The oneness of mind that Western authors and critics bring to their work on Africa says something about political power as well as educational policy. When "some group's knowledge [is defined] as the most legitimate, ... while other groups' knowledge hardly sees the light of day, [this] says something extremely important about who has power in a society" (Apple, 345). As most of the books covered in our study indicate, new generations are being offered a view of Africa that is allegedly authentic. Book reviewers mention time and again that the novel they are critiquing comes right out of today's news.

In considering the books under review here, the most disturbing question that arises is this: "Where is Africa in the minds of the authors?" Africa would appear to be situated on another planet. Even after five hundred years and all that has happened between Westerners and Africans, too many fiction writers have chosen to reinforce prejudices. This is in all probability an unwitting choice, but its pervasiveness links it with a long colonial and neocolonial history—a record in which cultural imperialism was as important as other forms of cultural domination. As we comment briefly about the contours of this history, and about imperialist children's literature, we can see the outlines of a book tradition that remains essentially unaltered—even in its most recent incarnation.

Colonialism and Colonialist Children's Fiction

Building an imperial-colonial structure in Africa was the work of various agents: e.g., slave-catchers, missionaries, explorers, empire-builders, colonial civil servants, soldiers, and propagandists. And their missions were interrelated, as Ethiopian emperor Tewodrus II wryly infers in his quip from the 1860s, "I know their game. First traders and missionaries, then ambassadors, then the cannon. It's better to get straight to the cannon" (Davidson, *The Search for Africa*, 13). Irrespective of faith or denomination, missionaries often saw their "civilizing-the-natives-mission" as in complete accord with forced labor, plantation profits, and the like. Even in the early days of chattel slavery, church agents were implicated in the monetary side of the infamous trade. Research by Abbe Jardin confirms that the church "was content to demand that slaves collected for America be first baptized, so that at least their souls might be saved. Otherwise the affair was thought regular enough ..." (Davidson, *African...*, 55). For performing the baptism, the bishop received a share of the export (slave) tax. In the 17th century "the baptismal tax ... was payable by the slave traders ... to the parish priest of Remedios and Benguela. After the 17th century when the slave trade had become an accepted institution ... the bishop secured 150 Reis [per head] of this tax for his own coffer."

Explorers in Africa were consistently at work from the late 1700s until the late 1800s, when the basic configuration of the continent became fairly well known. They came on map-making jaunts and other scientific quests. They were rewarded with honors and ceremonies in exchange for all the pleasant excitement their wanderings aroused in the folks back home.*

Empire-builders such as Cecil Rhodes, George Goldie, and Karl Peters depended on military support to ensure their hold on African territory and resources. Rhodes made millions from mining. Among other things, Goldie consolidated the companies that were bringing £300,000 worth of palm oil down the Niger River annually. Peters is credited with bringing under German rule the area that is now the independent state of Tanzania. He zealously set forth to rectify what he called a "deplorable state of affairs"—namely that "the German nation finds itself without a voice in the partition of the world which has been proceeding since the fifteenth century" (Rowell, 33).

Underlying all this activity was a set of assumptions that, according to historian Basil Davidson, became "thickened and compacted," assumptions that served as an ideological legacy. Among these assumptions was the notion that Africans were inherently and necessarily inferior to Europeans, that Africans were like "retarded children," incapable of growing up. They were deemed devoid of "civilization" because unequipped with

*From Britain came Livingstone, Speke, Burton, Baker, and Cameron. From Germany came Barth, Rohlfs, Nachtigal, Lenz, Junker, and Wissmann. From France came de Brazza and Binger; Serpa Pinto came from Portugal, Stanley from the United States, and Andersson from Sweden. (See The Scramble for Africa, c. 1870–1914 by Trevor Rowell. London: B.T. Batsford Ltd., 1986.)

European-style technology (i.e., railroads, telegraphs, etc.). Davidson writes:

> The cultures of Africa were seen as utterly closed off in their continental cul-de-sac; and it [was] ... barely questioned anywhere, that whatever good might accrue to Africa's peoples, whether in their ideas or organizations, would and must now be "done *to* them;" they could produce nothing useful of their own [*Search*, 13].

These self-serving myths surfaced repeatedly in books that were either written for or made available to children and young people. A succinct overview of this literature is available in Bob Dixon's *Catching Them Young, [vol.] 2*. What we refer to here are the major trends pinpointed by Dixon. The patterns are not dissimilar to those in books published in the 1980s and 1990s. Beginning with Daniel Defoe's *Robinson Crusoe* (1719), Dixon illustrates how many elements in the imperial tradition appeared in this novel. Racial hierarchies, for example, were assumed without question. Crusoe's slave, Friday, is admired to the degree that his appearance approaches the European standard. The slave "had the softness of an European in his countenance.... His hair was long and black, not curled like wool ... his nose small, not flat like the Negroes; a very good mouth, thin lips" (Dixon, 76).

Another feature that appears repeatedly in colonialist fiction (at least prior to the spreading influence of Darwin's *Origin of Species* published in 1859) is a reference to religion. White characters see themselves as under God's command to carry out "the white man's burden," and/or they thank God for creating Europeans unlike other "dreadful creatures" (as Defoe puts it) (Dixon, 76). A third quality is described by Dixon in these terms: "Violence and sadism of all kinds ... are rife in imperialist literature for children and usually it's cloaked in religion, racism, or patriotism, or combinations of these" (77–78). The way warring "tribes" kill and torture in early children's books shifts to a similar behavior among township blacks in modern works.*

A stock plot device is the willing sacrifice of the loyal native on behalf of the "master"—the same fate Friday suffers in *Robinson Crusoe*. This trait continues in twentieth-century novels, but by the mid-nineteenth century, slavery as an institution is being frequently condemned. Other changes include the introduction of the British public school into

---

*A township, as defined in these pages, is an area outside South African cities for the accommodation of Africans who work in the neighboring urban area.

colonialist stories and clashes among colonial powers in the English children's books (96).* A few quotations from the books of Edgar Wallace indicate the type of aspersions that were cast on Africans:

> ... there is no love in simple native men, save a love for their own and their bellies [*Keepers of the King's Peace* (1917)].

> Native folk ... are but children of a larger growth [*Keepers of the King's Peace* (1917)].

> "...black missionaries I will not endure."
> The Reverend Kenneth [a Liberian missionary] rose quickly, and accepted the situation with a rapidity which will be incomprehensible to any who do not know how thumbnail deep is the cultivation of the cultured savage [*Sanders of the River* (1911)].

Dixon quotes another passage that expresses Wallace's views of interracial marriage: "'Black is black and white is white, and all that is between is foul and horrible'" (103).

In addition to Defoe at one end of the continuum and Wallace, W.E. Johns, and Roald Dahl at the other, such writers as Frederick Marryat, W.H.G. Kingston, Charles Kingsley, Robert M. Ballantyne, G.A. Henty, H. Rider Haggard, Rudyard Kipling, and Hugh Lofting are covered in Dixon's brief overview of the imperialist tradition. His generalizations are essentially reaffirmed in Meena Khorana's introduction to *Africa in Literature for Children and Young Adults: An Annotated Bibliography of English-Language Books* (1994), as they are also largely validated in an earlier work: Nancy J. Schmidt's *Children's Books on Africa and Their Authors: An Annotated Bibliography* (1975).†

The latter book received severe criticism when it first appeared—that is, Schmidt was accused of being not sufficiently child-centered. Anne

*See also J.A. Mangan's "Noble Specimens of Manhood: Schoolboy Literature and the Creation of a Colonial Chivalric Code" in Imperialism and Juvenile Literature, ed. by Jeffrey Richards (Manchester, UK and NY: Manchester University Press, 1989).

†Other useful references include Nancy Schmidt's Supplement to Children's Books on Africa and Their Authors (1979); Meena Khorana's "Apartheid in South African Children's Fiction," Children's Literature Association Quarterly, 13:2, 52-56 (1988); Susan J. Hall's "What Do Textbooks Teach Our Children about Africa?', Interracial Books for Children Bulletin, 9:3 (1978); Ann Hedge and Ann Marie Davies' "Images of Africa in British History Texts," Interracial Books for Children Bulletin, 10:4 (1979); and two issues of Interracial Books for Children Bulletin that were primarily concerned with South Africa: Vol. 15: 7 & 8 (1984) and Vol. 16: 5 & 6 (1985).

Pellowski, writing in *The Horn Book Magazine*, was concerned because Schmidt did not explain how "children get accurate and authentic views of peoples." Pellowski states that "one is on shak[y] ground in attempting to describe the authenticity of fictional and folkloric works as perceived by children" (342). But Schmidt's contribution was in noting the way some authors who write about Africa perceive Africans. Her goal, she said, was "to convey whether the book contributes to an understanding of African people and whether an African viewpoint is conveyed in the book" (x). One can only be glad that she did not conform to the antiintellectual criterion described by Pellowski:

> Children's librarians ... are notoriously skeptical about research in the field of children's literature grounded *on facts* or statistics, rather than on direct experience with children [emphasis added]. A scholar wishing to influence them must take this into account [342].

Concerns about audience are to be expected, and in children's book circles the debate about readers and responsibility is generally connected with currents of political thought.

Readers and Social Responsibility

Reader response theory has amended the once-rigid ideas about young readers. According to a "reader response" approach, books offer a spectrum of possible readings; they are "response-inviting structures;" they are full of "blanks" that readers supply in relation to their own needs and backgrounds (Selden, 108–12). Children in particular can be viewed as unpredictable respondents since they come to a literary work not only with limited experience; they also have a limited and highly varied *reading* experience to draw upon, as well as varied socio-cultural group identifications. Peter Hunt writes:

> Unlike other forms of literature, which assume a peer-audience and a shared concept of reading (and which can therefore acknowledge, but play down, the problem of how the audience receives the text), children's literature is centered on what is in effect a cross-cultural transmission. The reader, inside or outside the book, has to be a constant concern, partly because of the adult's intermediary role, and partly because whatever is implied by the text, there is even less guarantee than usual that the reader will choose (or be able) to read in the way suggested [191].

This being said, however, authors still set the parameters of the readers' choices to a large degree, and author responsibility cannot be evaded.

Nor are the critics' assessments unimportant. By way of example, here is a statement about colonialist writer Hugh Lofting (author of the "Doctor Dolittle" books):

> Recently Lofting has come under attack for his use of words like "nigger" and "coon" and for his comical portrayals of the "savages" he encounters.... These lapses should not be allowed to spoil the books' real worth; their innocence, the lack of all whimsy, and the fact that Lofting was a genuinely original writer with an unusually inventive mind and a great gift for adventure [Moorehead, 609].

The critic in this case excludes Africans and people of African descent from her literary world as surely as does Lofting. Lofting's "inventive mind" served him in creating offensive, white supremacist scenes—a fact that cannot translate into "worth" for blacks, nor should they be deemed worthwhile by non-blacks. What Moorehead does in her appraisal of Lofting brings to mind what novelist John Killens observed about African Americans vis-à-vis the media: "The American Negro remains a cultural nonentity as far as books, television, movies and Broadway are concerned. It is as if twenty million Americans do not exist; twenty million people are committed to oblivion..." (quoted in Birtha, 59).

Fiction writers make choices as to what they will introduce, and those decisions cannot be lightly dismissed. Sociologist Joan Rockwell alludes to their significance:

> Narrative fiction is an indicator, by its form and content, of the morphology and nature of a society, just as the specific structure and function of the family in a society will be an indicator of how that society differs from others.
> Fiction, to be sure, is a social product; but it also "produces" society, because it has a normative effect on its members, perhaps especially in childhood [vii, viii].

From this premise it would be hard to argue that authors are exempt from social responsibility, yet children's writers continually make that exemption for themselves. Jean Little, for example, writes:

> I do not believe that writers have a responsibility to society. I believe our only responsibility is to be faithful to the vision each of us is given, however fragmentary and imperfect, of the book which has claimed us as its writer [79].

Little personifies the object she is creating and claims that "we have only to figure out where the book is crying out to go—and then take it there" (79). This overlooks the fact that writers and their material are to a degree produced by society and, as Rockwell explains, "[they] therefore necessarily contain information about it" (6).

If the books covered here are "crying out to go" somewhere, it is largely in the direction of white supremacy and historical misrepresentation. This is not to say that this is a conspiratorial action, but how can the writer shirk all responsibility? Juxtaposing African and European personalities and cultures—and then designating the former as of lesser quality—this comes about as countless decisions about character and plot are resolved.

Jean Little may be right when she insists that "memorable, moving books are not written from a sense of duty" (80), but it is equally true that racist books have been produced as a consequence of a *lack* of a sense of duty to the world's children. The history of imperialism has been too lengthy to suppose that this dilemma could be easily avoided, especially when Western peoples deny its very existence. In any case, there is no necessary conflict between craft and content. "Just because a writer is *engagé*," writes Chinweizu, et al., "...is no excuse for him to be a hack" (255). An African aesthetic accommodates both commitment and technique:

> Because in Africa we recognize that art is in the public domain, a sense of social commitment is mandatory upon the artist. That commitment demands that the writer pay attention to his [her] craft, that he not burden his public with unfinished or indecipherable works. It also demands that his theme be germane to the concerns of the community [252].

Society's concerns do not constitute a narrow and limiting "quarry for themes," says Chinweizu; it "is as big as all of the society and its history, its imagination and its future" (253).

In the process of understanding characterization, dialogue, plot, point of view, and theme as they affect African subject matter, it becomes obvious that the images produced have not been simple and harmless. The national origin of these images has been various, but they have generally been tinged with some idea of "race."

The S.A.-U.K.-U.S. Triangle

Three points in the triangle of neocolonialist fiction are easily identifiable as South Africa, Great Britain (U.K.), and the United States. The English-speaking world naturally shares its literary products, and this is especially true since publishing has now become a largely multinational business. Still, the unanimity expressed by writers, publishers, reviewers, bibliographers, prize jurors, and members of professional organizations regarding conceptions of Africa is both revealing and alarming. To turn attention to the much-discussed hegemony of the Western, industrialized nations, one need look no further than the children's literature about Africa.

In the first eight essays in this collection, we purposely examine novels that have the institutional apparatus of education and librarianship backing them up. The books have been elevated to preeminence by means of literary awards, "best book" committees, and the critical writings of known specialists in the field. Having had this boost from literary "gatekeepers," all the novels were easily accessible in the small, midwestern college town where we conducted our study (i.e., Iowa City, Iowa). And although the books were generically diverse (including adventure, fantasy, humor, and "problem" novels), they all said about the same thing. They all implied that the authors understood *what to expect* of Africans, or *what was good* for the African. Both mindsets are fraught with ill judgments and the influence of Apartheid. Whether originating in South Africa, the U.K., or the United States, the educational mission has been to treat Africa as the home of white settlers rather than the sovereign domain of its indigenous population. This reflects the ongoing neocolonial dynamic. Stephen Small describes its essence:

> Racialized barriers and boundaries were erected to secure political and economic goals; the former blocked black access to resources and power, while facilitating non-black access; the latter demarcated the acceptable terrain (political, economic, social) which could be traversed by black people, while keeping all terrains open to non-blacks [15].

Small adds that "racialized identities were the ideological terrain" that shaped interpretations of events. We argue that the "ideological terrain" of children's literature gives weight to the white supremacy myth and extends its lifespan.

Conclusion

Africa remains a sure-fire literary vehicle for Western writers—people who need an "exotic" setting for high adventure or a credible setting for environmental protectionism; a stage for minstrel-like antics or a highly-charged atmosphere in which to argue about government (or rather the Africans' doubtful capacity for self-government). What the fiction writers seem unable to reach beyond is the one-sidedness of colonialist thought. To move into a post–colonial era, concepts such as power-sharing, coexisting cultures, and mutual respect must find their way into the fictions that appropriate Africa as their setting. Steve Biko pleaded the multicultural cause for South Africa before his assassination at the hands of the police in 1977. The following is from the court record in 1976 when he was interrogated for his "one person, one vote" principles:

> ... a white child does not have to choose whether or not he wants to live with the white, he is born into it. He is brought up within white schools, white institutions, and the whole process of racism somehow greets him at various levels ... so whites are together around the privileges that they hold, and they monopolise this away from black society....
> This country looks, My Lord, like a province of Europe. ... It has got no relationship rootwise to the fact that it happens to exist in Africa.... [T]he black man here ... in the joint culture is going to sufficiently change our joint culture to accommodate the African experience. Sure, it will have European experience. ... We don't dispute that. But for God's sake it must have African experience as well [132, 131].

Works Cited

Apple, Michael W. "The Politics of a National Curriculum." In *Transforming Schools.* Ed. Peter W. Cookson Jr. and Barbara Schneider. New York: Garland Publishing, Inc., 1995; pp. 345–70.

Biko, Steve. *I Write What I Like.* (A selection of his writings edited by Aelred Stubbs C.R.) London: Heinemann, 1987 (first published in 1978).

Birtha, Jessie M. "Portrayal of the Black in Children's Literature." In *The Black American in Books for Children; Readings in Racism.* 2nd ed. Ed. Donnarae MacCann and Gloria Woodard. Metuchen, N.J.: Scarecrow Press, 1985; pp. 57–65.

Chinweizu, Onwuchekwa Jemie, and Ihechukwu Madubuike. *Toward the Decolonization of African Literature. Vol. 1: African Fiction and Poetry and Their Critics.* Enugu, Nigeria: Fourth Dimension Publishing Co., 1980.

Davidson, Basil. *African Awakening.* London: Jonathan Cape, 1955.

_____. *The Search for Africa: A History in the Making.* London: James Currey, 1994.

Defoe, Daniel. *Robinson Crusoe and A Journal of the Plague Year.* New York: Modern Library (Random House), 1948. (Originally published in 1719).

Dixon, Bob. *Catching Them Young (2): Political Ideas in Children's Fiction.* London: Pluto Press, 1977.

Feagin, Joe R., and Hernan Vera. *White Racism: The Basics.* New York and London: Routledge, 1995.

Hunt, Peter. "Narrative Theory and Children's Literature." *Children's Literature Association Quarterly* 9:4 (Winter, 1984–85): 191–4.

Khorana, Meena. *Africa in Literature for Children and Young Adults: An Annotated Bibliography of English-Language Books*. Westport, Conn., and London: Greenwood Press, 1994.

Little, Jean. "A Writer's Social Responsibility." *New Advocate* 3:2 (Spring, 1990): 79–88.

Lofting, Hugh. *The Story of Doctor Dolittle*. New York: Frederick A. Stokes, 1920. (Eleven additional "Dolittle" books were published between 1922 and 1952.)

Manteaw, E.S.A. "Letters: Western Media Bias." *West Africa* (July 31–August 6, 1995): 1191.

Moorehead, Caroline. "Hugh Lofting." In *Twentieth-Century Children's Writers*. 3rd ed. Ed. Tracy Chevalier. Chicago and London: St. James Press, 1989; pp. 608–9.

Pellowski, Anne. "Letters to the Editor." *Horn Book* 52:4 (August, 1976): 339.

Rockwell, Joan. *Fact in Fiction; The Use of Literature in the Systematic Study of Society*. London: Routledge & Kegan Paul, 1974.

Rowell, Trevor. *The Scramble for Africa (c. 1870–1914)*. London: B.T. Batsford Ltd., 1986.

Schmidt, Nancy J. *Children's Books on Africa and Their Authors*. N.Y.: Africana Publishing Co., 1975.

Selden, Raman. *A Reader's Guide to Contemporary Literary Theory*. Lexington: University of Kentucky Press, 1985.

Small, Stephen. *Racialised Barriers: The Black Experience in the United States and England in the 1980s*. London and New York: Routledge, 1994.

Wallace, Edgar. *Keepers of the King's Peace*. London: Ward, Lock, 1917.

_____. *Sanders of the River*. Garden City, N.Y.: Doubleday, Doran & Co., 1930. (Originally published as a book in 1911 by Ward, Lock.)

Animal Fantasy/
Human Animalness

Distortions of Kenyan Culture and History

Metamorphosis is an idea with strong appeal and age-old connections. The shape-shifter comes out of ancient mythology and enters the modern novel with its powers intact—in particular its capacity to enchant young readers. When Eric Campbell changes a human into a beast and a beast into a human in *The Year of the Leopard Song* (1992), he can be quite sure that he will hold his audience captive no matter what historical misrepresentations he weaves into the drama. The separation between human animalness and animal humanness can be drawn as a delicate line, and the fantasy writer has long been adept at tangling and untangling that line with spellbinding effects. However, in fiction about Africa, the beast has other connotations: the "beast" is the so-called cannibalistic African residing in an untamed landscape; also the "beast" is the beast of burden, the peon working happily in the fields of the European colonizer. These themes come into play as Campbell sketches a repugnant portrait of Black Kenyans and a noble delineation of a white settler family.

To understand why Campbell has created a work that demeans African character and extols neocolonialist exploitation, we can examine some of the clues in the book-jacket synopsis. The blurb states:

> When Kimathi embarks on a ritualistic journey to the peak of Mount Kilimanjaro, Alan [the white planter's son] sets out after him, determined to salvage their friendship and to find an answer to the recent mysterious happenings that have made him feel like a stranger in his homeland.

The mysterious happenings begin as soon as eighteen-year-old Alan Edwards returns from school in England and finds his childhood playmate, Kimathi, changed. Instead of being the companionable son of the household's cook, Kimathi has become the one chosen by the Chagga people to execute Alan in a sacrificial ritual. While in training for this murder, Kimathi shape-shifts into a leopard on several occasions and practices the skills that will make him a man-eater. Instead of direct cannibalism, Campbell runs the old stereotype through the metamorphosis myth, allowing an African-turned-animal to fulfill the hideous deed. In the end, Alan's father shoots him; in fact, everyone in the Chagga village (except the women and the young) is exterminated before the novel concludes. The region is once more "pacified" for imperialistic purposes:

> John Edwards and his family returned to the farm and tried to resume their lives. Gradually new workers [Africans] appeared, and the coffee slopes rang to the sound of voices once more [159].

The jacket synopsis refers to the salvaging of a friendship, the "ritualistic journey" of the Chagga youth, and the condition of being "a stranger in [one's own] homeland." Important and sensitive issues are contained in each of these plot strands. Looking first at the friendship loss, what is it that establishes initially the idea of lifelong friendship? We hear about the bond from Alan's viewpoint: "Whatever Kimathi was doing—whatever he had to do—could not destroy the bond they had between them. A bond built, cemented from the very early days of childhood, could not just vanish like this" (44). However, we hear nothing from Kimathi to confirm or deny this tie of friendship. The rich white settler and the deprived indigene supposedly share a relationship of trust and camaraderie, but one of many imperialistic tactics is to exploit another in the name of friendship. Kimathi's father has remained "a boy" throughout his entire life: the "houseboy" of the Edwards family. Alan observes him as "a small, dark figure," "a part of the family"; "[he was] always there, always the same, dependable and changeless, as warm and comforting and eternal in his presence as the house itself" (39). To be as steady as an inanimate object is to be classified a "friend"—a usable commodity in a colonial setting.

Kimathi's father has alerted young Alan to the fact that Kimathi has a different destiny: "The Kimathi you knew is no more. The boy is gone. Now the man must tread another path" (42). But the message does not penetrate. Alan believes implicitly that he is in charge and that when he finds Kimathi, together they will prove that "friendship and trust [are] stronger than ... magic ... stronger than race or color or culture" (44). Kimathi, it seems, will be assimilated into a "nobler," "friendlier" culture via Alan's tutelage. But at eighteen years of age, Alan must know that his security, based on whatever his parents have, has undercut and left Kimathi deprived and disadvantaged. As future heir of a coffee plantation, he must realize that his predecessors have unlawfully taken from Kimathi's father's father the land and all its wealth. His forebears have left Kimathi essentially disinherited. Moreover, the links between the two young men do not suggest even a casual acquaintance. There is no indication that they kept in touch while Alan was away in school. There is no visiting back and forth in each other's houses. Instead, Kimathi is taken for granted like the ever-present shadow that is his father's role in the Edwards' residence. And since a racial mix is taboo in the colonial milieu, what is the alleged friendship based upon other than Alan's conviction that he knows what is best for his African neighbor? To even fathom a condition of friendship, a condition of mutuality must be present; however, at every opportunity, Campbell creates a hierarchy of cultural models—an image of irrationality and depravity versus an image of intelligence and geniality. The "ritual journey" of Kimathi is a journey involving a murderous tradition.

Religion, Ritualism, and Cultural Arrogance

The religious subject matter in this novel is connected with the African characters exclusively. Yet, ironically, European missionaries have been the definers and describers of the religious culture, and in order to improve their own prospects, missionaries have painted African religions in purely pejorative terms. Campbell capitalizes on the notion that religion in Africa is anything but holy. On the contrary, it is monstrous. One of the most surprising elements in *The Year of the Leopard Song* is the bigotry that reduces particular creation myths to mindless magic, at best, or homicidal cults, at worst.*

Kimathi is off on a ritualistic journey, Alan is targeted as the sacrificial

---

Briefly, the myth is described by the narrator as follows: first only Spirit existed in the world and was built of air. He became bored and created the land and its creatures. Then he created tall trees and people came into being as they stepped out of the tree trunks with skin the color of bark. (Different ethnic groups came from different trees.) But one dark tree contained no life and from this the Spirit created black and gold blossoms; then the Spirit touched them to make the leopard (the perfect representative of the Spirit), and from the black trunk he created the Chagga people (guardians of the tree and the leopard). When a special mark appears on a Chagga (as in Kimathi's case since he has six fingers and six toes) he is to become the next guardian of the tree. And when the Spirit sings from the mountain, he is to follow the instructions in the song. If the tree dies, the Chagga people will die as well (74-75).

object in the ritual (i.e., the homicide victim), and the suspense of the
story centers on whether Alan will learn the truth about his would-be
"friend" in enough time to save his own life. But it is God, the Spirit,
who is orchestrating all this—who is luring Alan into the Chagga trap
with a magical song even as it guides the actions of the murderous divin-
ers with the "Leopard Song." The lyrics of the song, writes Campbell,
seep "down into the pores of [Kimathi's] skin":

> The Leopard runs alone.
> Run as the Leopard and hear its Song.
> The Leopard kills in darkness.
> Kill as the Leopard and be the Song.
> I am the Spirit. I am everywhere, everything.
> I am He. I am the sun and stars, the world and time.
> I am you and you are me.
> I am existence, eternal and changeless.
> I am creation. I decide [146].

In the climactic moment, the song gives the final instructions: "'Now it
is your time. The time of the Leopard. You, guardian of my spirit on
earth, now you must prove youself. The sacrifice approaches. Go now.
And kill'" (146). A mysterious struggle between good and evil is in the
making here, and the symbolism is in religious terms, in concepts relat-
ing to the cosmic and timeless.

In the hands of a Western writer, these mythic revelations incorpo-
rate grotesque images of the African and repeat the all-too-familiar missionary message: "Black is Evil, White is Good." Alan Edwards' father
presents this message explicitly while pondering how earlier generations
of whites have faced "the darkness and tribal violence" of Africa. He
explains what "darkest Africa" means: "A darkness not of the land itself—
of impenetrable jungle or unexplored vastnesses—but the darkness in the
hearts of men" (52). By linking the man-eating leopard and the dark-
hearted African until they literally become one, the author sets the stage
for European intervention—for a "civilizing mission" in this supposedly
cannibalistic land. And if this message is not sufficiently clear when the
white planter delivers it, we can listen as the African police chief describes
the horror of traditional culture: "'Tribal cults are deadly,'" says Chief
Makayowe. "'Kill each other if you wish—that's tribal.... But no one
touches the white man or his family. No one, or you will answer to me'"
(107). Even when Alan Edwards feels like a stranger in his own homeland, he can be assured that this African home is protected by the African police. Kenyan independence is really an extension of British rule,

according to Campbell's scenario. Sovereignty for Alan and his parents is implied as the Kenyan independence movement is belittled and misrepresented.

Homelands and Possession Rights

Campbell is working two tracks as he makes African traditions appear lethal while also presenting the Caucasian adolescent as in his "right place" in Africa. In the novel's opening pages we have this exultant description:

> The morning was clear and the sun already dazzling. He stood, luxuriating in the touch of the sun on his skin. He breathed deeply and gratefully the scent of Africa. A soft breeze was blowing in from the Kapiti Plain, and for Alan it carried memories on its breath: the acrid tang of acacia and loping giraffes; warm mist rising from lonely sand rivers; the smoke of cattle-dung fires; the sharp stench of lion; and the sweetness of sighing grass. The smell of the high veldt, the drug that draws all travelers back to Africa [4].

On the other hand, Alan comments that "England ... washes the life from you.... It encloses you in a prison of claustrophobia with its teeming people and killer traffic. He'd only needed a very tiny space to himself in England, but he hadn't been able to find it" (2). Alan has staked a psychological claim to the tropics, but no European tour of Africa is complete without its list of proverbial exotica. And to help the reading audience relish the latter, Campbell alludes to Alan's father in his great white hunter role. The living room of John Edwards displays prize trophies from his younger days: "A water buffalo gazed intimidatingly across the room at a gazelle, a lion glared down at a cheetah..." and so on (19). Still, a love of landscape does not produce the right of possession, and the author soon moves to a discussion of so-called "Mau Mau terror" to justify British rule.

First the author associates the Leopard Cult with the Kenyan independence movement by asserting, "The Leopard Cult was rising in this generation just as it had in the last. The tribes were demanding blood as they had in the 1950s" (52). Then Campbell interprets the history of the 1950s as it had been perceived by white settlers and officials:

> [The indigenous Africans] wanted their land back and the Mau Mau terror had been a means of achieving that end, the raids on isolated settlers' farms a well-organized campaign of harassment.

The murders of white families had been regrettable, of course, but the Mau Mau had simply been drawing attention to their cause. And not many whites had been killed after all....
So it had been a great storm in a very small teapot, hadn't it? The uprising had been crushed, Kenya had its independence ... and now it was all forgiven and forgotten ... [52-53].

The distortions of history in this flippant summary are many. To say that "not many whites had been killed" is to issue a true statement, but one that veils the horrors of this war as experienced by the Kenyan blacks. Official casualty figures for the three-year struggle include a total of 35 European civilians killed compared to 11,503 "terrorists" (i.e., independence activists) (Berman, 352). Members of the resistance movement who used the forests for shelter and a base of operations had no more than 1030 precision weapons, whereas the British used against them a Royal Air Force bomber formation, a division of African and British troops, 20,000 police officers, and a large cadre of administrative personnel. Both armored and artillery units were part of the colonial force.

This hardly warrants the phrase "storm in a teacup" if we take account of the African perspective. Moreover, 18,069 indigenous Africans were imprisoned without trial for so-called Mau Mau offenses, and 1,000 were eventually executed (Berman, 353).

While Campbell blithely conceals and minimizes the campaign that crushed the resistance, he directs the reader to sinister forces that "the worldly-wise dismissed as fantasy," forces that had to do with magic (53). As an example he cites a skirmish in which a Mau Mau attacker had been "slammed [with] three bullets" in the chest, but had metamorphosed into a leopard while in the final throes of death. This scene connects the alleged animalistic Africans within the independence movement and the animalistic antagonists in the 1990s setting. Mau Mau was described in colonialist propaganda as a disease to be stamped out (Berman, 354). Campbell seems to be retaining this mindset as he describes Kimathi and other Chaggas. (In fact, the name "Kimathi" recalls the actual name of a Mau Mau field commander, Dedan Kimathi, who eluded security forces until 1955 and was then captured and charged with illegal possession of firearms and ammunition; he was executed on those grounds.)

As in the 1950s colonial regime, so in the 1990s Campbell writes as if he has no consciousness of the displacement of Africans, or the race problems created by whites over the last five hundred years. The novel's narrator tells us that "'This was [Alan Edwards'] home. Africa was his home. Home was the place you ran to when everything else was crumbling. And he was as much a part of Africa as Kimathi and Njomo [Kimathi's father]. Though his skin was white he was African nevertheless" (43). This emotional plea is imbued with little credibility when we remember that "home" in this case means "coffee plantation" and the indigenous peoples were prohibited from cultivating coffee (Nafziger, 37). They had learned the skill of coffee-growing from the Germans, but the British proclaimed this activity illegal. For Kimathi and Njomo, "home" means being a peon in the white settler community—a cheap labor force. Instead of being allowed to produce export crops and improved cattle, African farmers were compelled by the colonial government to work on mountain roads and produce only the government-mandated crops that reduced indigenous economic development (Nafziger, 37). This is an ultimate form of dispossession. The British have defined themselves as among the world's most unabashed exploiters, and for Campbell to play the race card is a diversionary tactic. Alan's white skin is not the problem; his family's theft of African lands and livelihood—*that* is the problem.

Moreover, the underdevelopment of African peoples was blatant on the cultural as well as the economic plane. In 1936 the government was spending 33 times as much for the education of the European child as for the African. By 1951 this ratio had increased to 44:1 (Nafziger, 44). And when schooling was provided, the nature of the education was imperialistic. History and geography, writes Basil Davidson, "were taught from a racist standpoint: tending to show that whatever came from Europe was good or useful, and that whatever came from Africa was either the reverse or not worth studying" (82). White settler pressures upon education were continuous and explicit. In a government report in 1949, the white perspective was stated frankly: "Illiterates with the right attitude to manual employment are preferable to products of the schools who are not readily disposed to enter manual employment" (Nafziger, 44). What kind of "homeland" for Africans is implied in this report? Why is Campbell treating Alan as the underdog, the poor white settler who is feeling like a "stranger in his homeland?"

In effect, Campbell also ousts Africans from their "home," their right of possession, through the delineation of tyrannical characters. For example, Commander Sebastian Makayowe, the police chief, is almost apelike. He is compared to Idi Amin in his ruthlessness. Prisoners who have been in his jail on previous occasions scurry for cover, for they know "the bubbling volcano of rage that could surface at any capricious moment in an eruption of flying fists and boots and bellowed outrage" (48). Police work is carried on in this novel as a totally irresponsible endeavor. "In Moshi there was Tanzanian law and Makayowe's law. And Makayowe's law was the more feared." When Makayowe smashes the heads of drunks against the wall, he is just cleaning up "the human sewage that leaked constantly into his beloved town" and making way for "another batch [that] would be starting to build..." (50). He forces confessions from Africans using brutal, tyrannical means, while serving John Edwards and presumedly other planters as their lackey.

Instead of depicting a legitimate police service in the town of Moshi, Campbell gives us images of black-on-black violence. This portrayal only adds to the reader's impression that as a land base, Africa is best placed under an outsider's control. Similarly, the "myth of Mau Mau" was a widely circulated ideology lending further support to this theme. This myth can be described as a basic part of the novel's historical context, since point by point, Campbell seems to be embracing the components of the myth.

The Myth of Mau Mau

The colonial Kenyan government found itself in need of a legitimating myth after declaring a State of Emergency in 1952. Fearing the growth of a viable independence movement, official state violence escalated and needed justification. Some 27,000 Kikuyu, Embu, and Meru were detained while another 20,000 were deported from Nairobi to the reserves. In the detention camps, the people had no means of subsistence other than handouts supplied by the colonial government. These actions were taken against a largely unarmed civilian population and required explanation in Britain and the world at large. But through its monopoly power and access to the media, colonial authorities could disseminate an image of Mau Mau that would instill fear in any anticolonial sympathizers.

Before we discuss WaChui, the primary spiritual leader of Kimathi's community, we need to consider the elements in the myth of Mau Mau in some detail and to note how the myth links religious and political power. According to historian Bruce Berman, the myth of Mau Mau can be summarized in the following general terms:

Mau Mau was a form of mass psychosis involving an atavistic rejection of modern civilization and an attempt to revert to a degraded savagery. It found its roots in the secretive and suspicious 'forest psychology' of the Kikuyu people, and its immediate causes in a breakdown of self-control and the constraints of tribal tradition. ... The Mau Mau organization itself was a fanatic religious cult created and cynically manipulated by a group of unscrupulous politicians motivated by a lust for power, the most important of whom was Kenyatta. Through the use of bestial oaths and magic these leaders sought to turn their followers into murderous automatons, complete pariahs from all decent relations and values [353].

The primary motivation behind Mau Mau, according to Berman, was the ouster of Europeans and Asians from the colony. Links between socioeconomic factors and the Mau Mau movement were disavowed in the myth circulated by colonial forces. In the 1952-53 trial of Kenyatta, the judge dismissed Kenyatta's list of Kikuyu land grievances with the remark: "'I gather grievances have nothing to do with Mau Mau, and Mau Mau has nothing to do with grievances'" (355). The Prosecution argued that Kenyatta was developing a religious cult (Berman, 355).

In Campbell's novel, WaChui, the ageing "Watcher of the Tree, is the representative of atavism. He orchestrates the regressive actions of the Chagga community, insisting that the death-bestowing ritual that targets Alan Edwards is of the Spirit. In an argument with police chief Makayowe, he makes these statements:

I tell [the Chagga people] nothing. ... What they do is what the tribe has always done. The Spirit tells them what they must do, not I. ... We have no choice. The Spirit gives us no choice.... We have to follow the path we are given.... Let things take their course. ... Why do you [Makayowe] interfere? This is tribal, stay out of it [105–6].

On the one hand, WaChui is depicted as just an old, benighted, priest-like figure; perhaps his destructive "religious" beliefs are due in part to senility and in part to cultural throwbacks. But on the other hand, the description of the ritual is decidedly political: the Chagga men "removed their clothes—the hated white man's uniform of shirts and shorts. They rolled them neatly and ... later they would burn them, the symbols of their subjection, of their taming by another race" (59). Instead of the Spirit, it is anti–European agitation that is at work; in short, African tradition and anticolonial politics are overlapping evils that warrant swift eradication. As in the nineteenth century, the missionary hysteria about alleged African mysticism is proving politically expedient (whether in the 1950s trial of Kenyatta or in a novel for the young in the 1990s). Implicit in the myth of Mau Mau is the idea that Africans want to drive out Europeans. Stated openly in Campbell's novel is the similar idea that Africans are loaded with race prejudice against whites. This turns history on its head, but it is a much-used imperialistic tactic.

The Black Racism Myth

When Alan Edwards returns from England and finds the atmosphere altered on his father's coffee plantation, he puzzles over the possible causes. First he believes that the people may be shy because he has established his ties with Great Britain. But he says he "didn't really convince himself" that this was the cause. Instead he shares this thought:

> There were things out there, beyond the farm fence, that no expatriate could ever know about; not even one like Alan, who had been born here and lived almost all his days here. Africans extended the warm hand of friendship to pull you in, but they didn't pull you in all the way. Only as far as they wanted you to come. Some doors would always remain closed though you knocked on them to the end of time [18].

Alan has apparently forgotten that even the "door" to growing a coffee crop was closed to Africans prior to the struggle for Kenyan independence.

Racism is introduced again when Alan turns to Kimathi's father for answers about the changed social climate. Njombo tries to persuade Alan to leave temporarily because he has returned at "a time of magic. ... A time for the black man, not the white" (41). When communication is at a low ebb, it is (according to this scenario) black exclusiveness that results in a widening gap of racial disharmony and misunderstanding.

Alan claims the moral high ground when he alludes to his own freedom from racism in contrast to Njombo's prejudice. Alan repeats the servant's statement: "'A time of magic. A time for the black man, not the white. ... Well, there were things stronger than magic. Stronger than race or color or culture'" (44). Friendship and trust, says Alan, are stronger. And as the scene ends, Alan hears "the harsh, rasping cough of a leopard"—a symbolic clue, perhaps, that leopard-man-Kimathi is not to be the friend that Alan idealistically believes in.

Conclusion

The many strands of neocolonial thought in Campbell's novel result perhaps from the author's experiences in the colonialist milieu of Africa. We are told on the book's cover that "most of his working life [was] spent in Papua New Guinea and East Africa, where he lived in the shadow of Mount Kilimanjaro." His own indoctrination, given such circumstances, may have left him ill-prepared to address African history and culture in unbiased terms. However, what accounts for the support given *The Year of the Leopard Song* by literary critics?

According to historian Lasine Kaba, "old myths about Africa and Africans as being 'primitive' and 'savage' have not vanished." He cites historian Basil Davidson's metaphor about these old myths—namely, that "they have retained a kind of underground existence, have settled like a layer of dust and ashes on the minds of large numbers of otherwise thoughtful people and are constantly being swirled about" (Kaba, 43–44). Certainly the "dust and ashes" of the "savagery" myth extend backward in time in American literary history. In a 1902 novel that also singles out the leopard as a symbol of evil—Thomas Dixon's *The Leopard's Spots*—Dixon is candid about his Negrophobia. He writes that the "[Negro] is a menace ... throwing the blight of its shadow over future generations, a veritable Black Death for the land and its people"; the Negro, according to Dixon, was "a beast to be feared and guarded" (quoted in Fredrickson, 280). Surprisingly, the beast-man metamorphosis is not mentioned in either the *Booklist* or the *Voya* reviews, even though this point is so central to the plot of the novel. Instead, reviewers center their attention on the friendship theme. The boys lives have been "intertwined" writes Chris Sherman for *Booklist* (416–7). Alan Edwards follows "his childhood friend" writes Mary Chelton, "little realizing that he is [facing] a ritualistic death at a transformed Kimathi's hand" (275).

An "engrossing," suspenseful tension also appeals to these reviewers, and Mary Chelton generalizes about what she calls the novel's underlying point: "the mystery of Africa itself" (275). She notes that European residents of Africa, "despite their feeling more 'African' than European," are still unaware of this "mystery of Africa." Chelton's concerns seem to rest with the European side of the equation—that is, she concludes with the comment that "the book offers insights into what Africans of European descent can feel like." The feelings of indigenous Africans—whose lands, wealth, and future destinies have been either appropriated or aborted—are not mentioned. Additionally, neither the Western author nor the Western critic appears interested in halting the age-old stereotype of the threatening (the implicitly evil) African. Nor is the world of colonial exploitation analyzed, even when the novel focuses on the issue in its climactic moments. In *The Year of the Leopard Song*, all the males in the Chagga village are wiped out, all the women and children abandon their homes, and the coffee planter, John Edwards, resumes his life with a growing corps of new field laborers: "The coffee slopes rang to the sound of voices once more" (159).

According to historian Lansine Kaba, what the West disallows is an image of Africa in which the general laws of progression and rational processes apply. A dynamic, evolving society is incompatible with colonial rule or neocolonial influence (48). At least potentially, "Africa's uneven relations with the outside world," says Kaba, could heighten mass consciousness and lead to radical change (50). This is reason for hope, but what needs to be added here is that *the education of children through literature must change as well*. Otherwise, the progress will be undone—a new generation will be fed books such as *The Year of the Leopard Song* and fear that African "primitiveness" threatens both them and their world.

Works Cited

Berman, Bruce. *Control & Crisis in Colonial Kenya: The Dialectic of Domination*. London: James Currey; Nairobi: Heinemann Kenya; Athens: Ohio University Press, 1990.
Campbell, Eric. *The Year of the Leopard Song*. San Diego: Harcourt Brace Jovanovich, 1992.
Chelton, Mary. Rev. of *The Year of the Leopard Song*. *Voya*, 15:5 (December, 1992).
Davidson, Basil. *Modern Africa*. London and New York: Longman, 1983.
Fredrickson, George. *The Black Image in the White Mind: The Debate on Afro-American Character and Destiny, 1817–1914*. New York: Harper and Row, 1971. Reprint, Middletown, Conn.: Wesleyan University Press, 1987.
Kaba, Lansine. "Historical Consciousness and Politics in Africa." In *Black Studies: Theory, Method, and Cultural Perspectives*. Ed. Talmadge Anderson. Pullman: Washington State University Press, 1990; pp. 43–51.
Nafziger, E. Wayne. *Inequality in Africa: Political Elites, Proletariat, Peasants and the Poor*. Cambridge: Cambridge University Press, 1988.
Sherman, Chris. Rev. of *The Year of the Leopard Song*. *Booklist*, 89:4 (October 15, 1992).

Traditional African Cultures in Juvenile Novels

Dysfunctional or Evolutionary?*

Western cultures and traditional African cultures are often placed in contrasting relationships in books for the young. The adjacency of these cultures is a purposeful contrivance, a way to highlight differences between so-called "old" and "new" worlds. For European and Euro-American authors, the purpose is usually to promote the "modern" and to suggest that without Western assistance Africa is eternally stalled in a cultural-political rut. Children's writers Mary Louise Clifford and Lesley Beake come to their task with this decidedly Western outlook and collection of biases. Yet books by these authors were written approximately twenty years apart, and the African world is depicted as less threatening in Beake's *Song of Be* (1993). Clifford apparently has little interest in toning down a conventionally anti–African message; or perhaps her colonialist stance is the only position she has ever had access to.

Both Clifford (an American) and Beake (a Scot) are writers of textbooks as well as novels: Clifford authored the *Noble and Noble African Studies Program* for high school students, and Beake devised learning materials for the San (Bushman or Ju/'hoan) peoples of the Kalahari Desert. Clifford was an American Foreign Service employee in Lebanon from 1949 to 1951 and, after that, the wife of a United Nations economic advisor in Africa and elsewhere. Beake resides in South Africa and has worked in Namibia as a teacher. As we examine Clifford's novels, *Salah of Sierra Leone* (1975) and *Bisha of Burundi* (1973), we will see how unabashedly imperialistic a Western writer could be in the 1970s. When we turn to Beake's *Song of Be*, we notice some of the same underlying assumptions but at a more subliminal level.

This essay was originally published in The Journal of African Children's and Youth Literature, *vol. 6 (1994/95). It is reprinted here in a slightly expanded form and with the permission of* JACYL.

Salah

Western book critics frequently join with European and American fiction writers in a common perception of African life. A reviewer of *Salah of Sierra Leone* reported that the tale was about "actual political events" (Johnson, 52). Judy Johnson recommended the novel as "a readable and enjoyable way to absorb political and social facts" (52). Similarly, in the *Horn Book* Paul Heins maintains that "the background [is] based on actual events" (55). Clifford's fictional exercise "well-embodies," says Heins, "the struggle between tribal loyalties and the vigorous innovations of twentieth-century African life" (55). These "actual facts" are really impressions directed at the Euro-American reader and geared to manipulate this gullible audience.

"What position do you play?" (1) This is the question that opens the novel and also serves as an introduction of Salah. The author seems interested in the welfare of the boy, but in order to understand the connotations behind the question, "What position do you play?" it is important to examine the "role-play" of the various invented characters. How are they juxtaposed? The headmaster, Mr. McLellan, waits impatiently for Salah's answer:

> "Can you run?"
> "Yes, Sir," Salah said.
> "Can you play defence?"
> "Yes, Sir."
> "Ever play goalie?"
> "Yes, Sir."
> McLellan sighed softly. What a typically African reaction, he thought.
> "Well, we'll try you in the forward line until we see what you can do" [2].

The headmaster's remark, "What a typically African reaction," positions him as a colonialist; from his perspective, only Africans (illiterates) act this way or that way. Clifford does not contradict this attitude but instead misrepresents the culture and history of both the Mendes (Salah's ethnic group) and the Creoles (the people represented by Luke Taylor, Salah's closest friend). The Mendes are a capable and very determined people. Salah would not have needed foreigners in order to learn how to give a simple, respectful answer to an elder. Nor would he have to think about whether he should speak truthfully about what he could or could not do. We have already read that he was one of the best athletes in his former school in Pendembu. The author dabbles unconvincingly in Mende traditions when she places Salah in that milieu and when she manuevers the plotline to elevate the Creoles at the expense of the Mendes. She describes how the schoolboy, Salah, is at the mercy of a tyrannical and cruel father but is drawn toward the "better" way of life of the Creoles. Luke's Creole mother helps Salah with his studies, even supplying the needed reading glasses; Salah's father heaves the glasses out the window. Luke enjoys visits to a free public library; Salah is denied a library card by his father and can only obtain one surreptitiously. Luke's father is upright in his actions vis-à-vis the 1967 election campaign; Salah's father is an army sergeant who is implicated in political corruption and election fraud.

This novel attempts to explain to young Euro-Americans the politics of post-colonial Africans and African leadership (in this case, the leadership of Sir Albert Margai, the Prime Minister in 1967 and a Mende by ethnicity). Unfortunately, the writer does not give enough information for the readers to understand the background of the real protagonist, Sir Albert, whom she criticizes as corrupt, dictatorial, and nepotic. "What position do you play?" connotes the political struggle of an election campaign in which Clifford makes her own position clear. She uses Luke Taylor as her mouthpiece: "They've [the Mendes] had their chance. They've been running things ever since the British put Sierra Leoneans in the cabinet way back in 1951. And look at the mess things are in" (57).

To understand the misinformation embedded in this bit of dialogue, we need to take a brief look at modern Sierra Leonean history. In March of 1967 the Governor General of Sierra Leone, Sir Henry Lightfoot Boston and others (including Siaka Stevens, whom the Governor General had appointed Prime Minister) were placed under house arrest. The Force Commander, Bridgadier Lansana, a Mende, declared martial law and purported to nullify the election. But before this election (the second in Sierra Leone after Independence) there had been a lot of accusations and bitterness between the leaders of the SLPP (Sierra Leone People's Party) and Siaka Stevens, leader of the APC (All People's Congress). Stevens had objected to the decisions of the constitutional conference in London and refused to sign the "Independence" document, and the APC frequently attacked the government of Sir Albert Margai over alleged extravagance and corruption. In the novel Luke expands upon his grievances: "[Sir Albert is] greedy, and he's all out for Sir Albert. He's gotten rich in office while the country is practically bankrupt" (57). The ethnic divide displayed in this novel, the hate and resentment, was not part of the norm during the Prime Ministership of Sir Milton Margai, Sir Albert's predecessor and brother. Nor were political party supporters divided along purely ethnic lines. Stevens was not a Creole and the APC was not exclusively a Creole political party; neither was the SLPP a Mende party. All the political parties were a mix of Mende and Temne ethnic groups (the largest) plus at least twelve other different peoples and languages. Clifford over-simplifies when she "positions" Mende characters in the pro-Albert camp and treats them as contemptible, while making the Creoles anti-Albert and the victims of Sir Albert's nepotic dictatorship.

In a scene in Salah's school, Clifford sets up the idea that ethnic differences make Africa all but ungovernable. The boys in his history class nearly come to blows as they discuss current events. The teacher, Mr. Demerish, serves as Clifford's mouthpiece as she conveys her contempt for Africa and its traditions. An extended quotation is given here in order to let the political perspective in this novel speak for itself. A class member starts off the debate:

> "If the British and French had drawn the boundaries differently, we wouldn't have all this trouble."
> "How would you change it?" Demerish asked.
> "We Africans should redraw the boundaries to suit ourselves."
> "What would you do in Sierra Leone? Give the Susa country to Guinea? The Vai and Kono to Liberia? That's where they came from originally."
> "Why should we give anything to Liberia? Let Liberia give us all her Vai and Kono area!"
> "Fat chance!"
> "How about the Mende? They weren't even in Sierra Leone when the Portuguese first came in the fifteenth century," Demerish reminded his class. "They all migrated into Sierra Leone in the last three hundred years."
> "Really? Where did they come from?"
> "Well, the Mende language is one of the Mande dialects, part of the big language family of the Upper Niger River basin. Presumedly the Mende came from that region originally."
> "Send all the Mende back to Mali," shouted an enthusiastic Temne lad. "Then the Temne would be the biggest tribe in Sierra Leone again, and we could run things!"
> A dozen Mende boys sprang to their feet as a roar of assent and dissent greeted this suggestion. Demerish had to stride into the middle of the room and pound on his desk to restore order. "You see," he pointed out when he could be heard again, "You can't even agree among yourselves. The government the British left you may not be the best system for solving your problems, but it was the best we could devise to give every group a fair chance" [85-6].

It is important to note how carefully Clifford plays her European colonial mindset in this charade. She ends the chapter with condescending remarks about African leadership:

> "It isn't working well now," protested Salah.
> "Not as well as we'd like," Demerish agreed. "Hopefully African leaders will work out more satisfactory arrangements as time goes by. But in the meantime, the Sierra Leone constitution is your natural law, and elections are to be held next month according to that law."
> "Do you think that they can be fair elections under a state of emergency, Sir?" Salah asked.
> Demerish studied the boy thoughtfully. "I hope so, Salah. I'm fearful for the country if they are not" [86].

That the boys cannot agree among themselves in this scene dramatizes ethnic divisions without revealing the complex manipulations of the British against the protectorate. Moreover, the actual ethnic and cultural identities in language and other traditional features indicate that Guinea, Sierra Leone, and Liberia were once one country—a country comprised of the same different ethnic groups found today in these three nations. To suggest inevitable conflict is to mislead and to play the divide-and-conquer game that characterizes imperialist incursions.

The orchestration of the love-hate relationship between Creoles and protectorate people was elaborately conceived at the time of the Temne-Mende War of 1898, and Clifford makes use of this history in implying that Africans cannot agree among themselves. The rationalization is constructed of convenient half-truths and negative innuendoes.

While political history is a muddle in Salah's story, the religious dimensions of Sierra Leonean life are depicted in a bad light through direct comparisons. For example, the Mende's God is said to be a "God far beyond the reach of mortal man," whereas the Christian God is "a bulwark," "a fortress," "a shelter"—a vital force in human experience (39). "There was a Mende God, of course," writes Clifford, "...but one only heard about Ngewo briefly from time to time" (39). Then Clifford continues with a trivialization of "lesser spirits," "ritual ceremonies," and the role of ancestors.

Her most direct condemnation, however, is reserved for the Poro society. Westerners often try to find out about "secret societies" but end up believing a mish mash of exaggerated stories. Clifford introduces Poro when Salah's father is accused of election improprieties and arrested. Members of the Poro society suspect that Salah has been an informer and plan to put him on trial in the Poro "court," a trial that would probably include a "trial by ordeal" (drinking deadly sasswood or walking on hot coals). This description of Poro seems more in keeping with stories Clifford might have been told by children than with any research on the subject. For a start, people who were given sasswood potions were those suspected of witchcraft, and it was believed that when they drank it, if they were members of the cult they automatically began to confess. As for the burning coals, certain persons did dance on broken bottles, not on burning charcoal, and this was done mostly for entertainment. On the question of divulging Poro secrets to noninitiates, no one would take the author seriously on this point except her Euro-American publisher, critics, and readers. Anthropologist K.L. Little notes that "discussion of Poro matters, even when superficial, with a nonmember, and particularly a European, is regarded as a serious offence" (14).

Aside from the author's failure to grasp the complex social and cultural meanings imbued in the Poro society, various manners, attitudes, and relationships are misrepresented. For example, Luke replies to Salah's question, "How did you talk your mother into letting you come?":

> Oh, she can't treat me like a complete baby. How am I going to learn anything sitting around the house? When she said I should stay home, I asked what Pa had said. He would have told her if he'd thought I shouldn't go down. What harm can it do just to go downtown? [121].

Luke may be a spoiled brat, but one thing about Creoles, they do discipline their children even if he/she is the only child. And irrespective of ethnicity, youngsters in Sierra Leone at the time this novel was written generally showed regard for parents and those older than themselves. This was true among the rich and poor, the educated and illiterate. Luke's sulky retort is entirely unlikely. Elsewhere Mrs. Taylor is described in terms that imply a racist bias in Salah. The narrative explains:

> Even though [Salah] didn't know what to expect, he sensed her motherly warmth. Her copper-brown skin, so much lighter than his own, immediately identified her mixed Creole blood, and of course there was the European dress she was wearing.... He knew that he instinctively liked and trusted this outgoing woman [8].

It is unlikely that a Creole woman would have been flattered by this description.

As for Salah's own family members, there seems to be no love, no warm feelings. His father, as we mentioned above, was exceedingly abusive. His grandmother "peered at him from white-filmed elderly eyes" and addressed him brusquely: "Why, Salah! What are you doing here? ... Where's your Pa? ... Is he mixed up in this revolution thing...?" (138). No Sierra Leonean grandmother would interrogate a beloved and long-absent grandchild in this way without putting herself to shame in the entire community. She would have suspended whatever she was doing, given him a good wash, prepared food for him, and informed the community of his arrival. She would not have prejudged the boy's father and made sarcastic remarks about him. According to Clifford, "[grandmother] turned away contemptuously" and chided the boy's father: "Just chasing shadows, he is. Always thinking he's going to get something for nothing!" (139). When questioned by Mrs. Taylor about his mother, Salah replies, "I don't have a ma" (9). This seems to be an expression of a Westerner's hysteria about the one-parent family; Salah's mother is alive and well and living in the region where Salah was born. In Sierra Leonean culture, this important person would not be removed either psychologically or emotionally from the extended family circle. Clifford is creating one excuse after another to tarnish the character of a people she knows hardly anything about.

In the biographical note about Clifford at the back of the book, we learn that her graduate work was being "directed toward a better understanding of how children acquire attitudes toward people in other cultures" (186). The irony is that people like Clifford are institutionalizing negative attitudes, a fact that is similarly apparent in the novel that preceded *Salah* by two years, *Bisha of Burundi*.

Bisha

When reading Clifford's *Bisha of Burundi*, one is haunted by a question: What evolutionary process must Africans go through as they approach the twenty-first century in order to be emancipated from the insults, stereotypes, and misrepresentations that have accumulated over preceding centuries?

"In 1962, [Burundi] became an independent constitutional monarchy with the traditional Tutsi *Mwami* as King. The monarchy was overthrown in 1965 by a group of army officers, and an army captain declared himself president of the new republic" (viii). Clifford supplies this background to her main storyline and adds that a civil war broke out in 1972 between the Hutus (the majority tribe) and the Tutsis (the minority that migrated from the upper Nile region and imposed its rule several centuries prior to the time frame of this narrative).

Having established the all-too-familiar "coup" history, the author proceeds with her coming-of-age tale about a Tutsi girl—an adolescent who must choose between continuing her schooling or agreeing to the marriage plan arranged by her parents. The scenario brings mixed images to the minds of those familiar with what happened on the continent (the coups and counter-coups) in the 1960s and beyond. Like *Salah of Sierra Leone*, *Bisha* is the story of a teenager in a country that has been milked dry by colonial exploitation. Bisha is caught between many conflicts, between cross-cultural struggles and multiple intrigues in the social, political, and economic spheres.

The political machinations are propelled largely by ambition. Bisha's grandfather is *chef de colline* (chief of a cluster of families) but will soon need a successor. Bisha's father expects this position, and her mother is the power behind her father—a veritable Lady Macbeth! To ensure the succession, Bisha's mother plots to marry her off to the province's party secretary (Burundi is a one-party state), and this will ensure political advantages for the secretary. Since Bisha's grandfather's nephew works in the controller's office in the Finance Ministry, marriage to Bisha will give the secretary access to the highest levels of government. Bisha's desire for further education and a career as a teacher are dismissed by her mother as unworthy of a hearing. Her father is sympathetic but spineless and indecisive on all questions that concern the family or the community.

If we put aside our prejudices about race, culture, and modern development—if we reflect upon our own adolescence and the needs of young adults—then Bisha's situation can be seen as not unique. The global adolescent character is recognizable, except that being an African, Bisha inherits all the negative trappings and impediments that Euro-Americans typically associate with the African. But Clifford largely ignores the realities that come with this stage of life—the traumas that prove frustrating to the child-adult, the parents, and the teachers.

What the reader might have been allowed to see of this period (when emotions produce either an exasperating or a joyous transition) is obscured by Clifford's tendency to heap blame upon alleged African backwardness. The ordeal of Bisha is compounded by the author's obsession to recreate eighteenth- and nineteenth-century tribal stereotypes, traditional characters who suffocate the child-adult. Caught in a milieu of decadence, Bisha listens to her father declare arbitrarily: "Your mother and I and my father and my brothers and their wives have all discussed what we feel would be good for you now that you are finishing the mission school, and we have reached agreement that you should marry" (70). Unlike child-adults in a modern Western setting, Bisha is refused the right to self-discovery—denied the privilege of searching out new ideas and experiences beyond the parameters of home and family. The urge to risk dangerous experimentation (common among adolescents), the urge to test the limits of one's strengths and weaknesses—these are all to be denied Bisha by her parents, who in the estimation of the novelist are not qualified for modern parenthood.

Clifford employs two central characters as conveyors of her dominant theme. First, the Belgian, Sister Benedicte, represents an all-knowing, all-perfect, all-compassionate "educator" who comes to continue colonial rule where her male counterparts left off. And second, Bisha, the wide-eyed innocent, has dangling before her all the new Western attractions that Western education, via a Catholic mission, can offer. The author uses divisive ploys to alienate the young Bisha from her culture, her parents, and her beliefs. "'You must not drink the water from the stream in the valley,' says Sœur Benedicte, 'for it is not clean and carries all sorts of germs into your body'" (15). But the stream is the only water source available. For decades the Belgian colonizers never cared about the health and welfare of these people. They could have built a reservoir and constructed water pipes to provide pipe-clean drinking water. Burundi was a Belgian colony from 1916 to 1962, and there was plenty of time and cheap labor for developing mobile health units in rural areas. Why is it that after Independence, there is this great urge to educate and modernize? Why the sudden focus upon young African women, who had been there all along while the men were subjected to physical and psychological abuse?

While depicting Burundi as a chaotic mess that needs saving from itself, Clifford concentrates on the female characters, setting up a plotline that allows her to comment on women's issues. Bisha's mother and the chief nun are polarized as representatives of the dysfunctional and constructive societies, respectively. Chimpaya (Bisha's mother) responds to another relative who asks if Bisha will like marrying a man so much older (the Secretary is a widower with three children); she says: "Like it? ... What has liking got to do with it? Good Tutsi daughters marry whom their parents choose, as you and I did" (36). Chimpaya blames education and foreign influences for her daughter's assertiveness and opposition to the arranged marriage. "*That's* what comes from all this book learning and those foreign teachers with their strange ideas!" (95). The foreign teachers, however, are the novelist's heroes. At the outset we are prepared for their positive role as the narrative explains: "At school she was Bisha—the only Bisha—and the sisters made her feel that what was best for Bisha mattered to them" (8). With this kind of support, Bisha excels as a scholar, winning every prize that the school offers. Her romantic interest, a college-bound scholar named Thomas, reinforces the positive connection between schooling and individualism. He describes approvingly how a relative "learned in school that everyone had a right to decide what he should do with his own life" (43).

Besides the nuns and Chimpaya, two other women are polarized for the sake of social commentary: Rubebe, Bisha's aunt, and Tangishaka, her sister-in-law. The former represents Western ideas about marriage and female self-determination; the latter typifies the alleged passivity and mental dullness of traditional African women. Tangishaka is so dependent on others that she resembles an infant. She is apparently minus a consciousness of her own. Rubebe teaches Bisha about a principled relationship with a man—a love-centered companionship. Her own husband died young, but Rubebe has refused to follow tradition; she has rejected polygamy and marriage to one of her brothers-in-law. She prefers eternal loyalty to her deceased spouse and economic independence, although she is barely making enough as a basket weaver to support herself and her aging parents. Clifford uses Rubebe to help strengthen Bisha's resolve to run away to middle school, if necessary, and put herself under the protection of the nuns. This is the course of action proposed by Thomas, who asks Bisha to marry him and become a Catholic, as well as follow her dream of becoming a teacher. "'You mean that it would be all right to join the church just to go to school?'" asks Bisha (129). "'It didn't trouble [the priests] one bit,' according to Thomas. '... once you were baptised, you had your whole life to figure out where you stood with God.'" And Thomas adds that "'...even if you never were much of a believer yourself, your children would have a Christian upbringing'" (129). So much for Western intellectual honesty.

Clifford puts disparaging remarks about women in the dialogue assigned to the male characters, making the novel appear sensitive to women's issues. Also she clearly opposes the role restrictions imposed on girls and women. But a purely Western variety of feminism is like other types of hegemonic imperialism. The best works in feminist scholarship are typically studies that reveal some consciousness of the intersection of race, gender, and class. But as Chandra Mohanty notes, "assumptions of privilege and ethnocentric universality ... characterize a sizable extent of western feminist work on women in the third world" (63). An analysis of "sexual difference" often leads to a supposed "third world difference," and in "the production of this 'third world difference' ... western feminisms appropriate and colonize ... the lives of women in these countries." With a homogeneous notion of the oppression of women, Westerners contrive a group image of the "average third-world woman," according to Mohanty. Essentially this group image is as follows:

> This average third-world woman leads an essentially truncated life based on her feminine gender (read: sexually constrained) and being 'third world' (read: ignorant, poor, uneducated, tradition-bound, religious, domesticated, family-oriented, victimized, etc.). This ... is in contrast to the (implicit) self-representation of western women as educated, modern, as having control over their own bodies and sexualities, and the 'freedom' to make their own decisions [65].

Bisha of Burundi has all the earmarks of the colonizing "feminist." While Clifford may be truly sensitive to sexism in Africa as elsewhere, she is not aware of African female networking, group action, assertiveness, and dynamic functioning within the group.*

The old imperialist pattern of manipulation of tribal leaders is similar to the pattern put into play in Clifford's novels. The difference is that the Euro-American "feminist" (liberal/conservative) is directing her efforts toward women and young people in order to maximize the process of Western hegemony—to deal a blow from which Africans cannot easily recover.

Be

Lesley Beake, author of *Song of Be*, is of a later generation than Clifford and does not follow Clifford in setting up cultural practices for the purpose of

*In 1929, tens of thousands of Igbo and Ibibio women challenged the corrupt members of the Native Courts, the British-controlled judicial system. The women's behavior was in accord with traditional patterns: "much noise, stamping, preposterous threats and a general raucous atmosphere..., all part of the institution of 'sitting on a man'." (See Judith Van Allen's "'Sitting on a Man': Colonialism and the Lost Political Institutions of Igbo Women," Canadian Journal of African Studies 4:2, 1972.) The women did not expect to be hurt, as they were following culturally appropriate actions, but fifty were killed and fifty wounded when the police opened fire on them. No men were even injured in this political action. (See Susan Z. Andrade's "Rewriting History, Motherhood, and Rebellion: Naming an African Women's Literary Tradition," Research in African Literature, 21:1, April, 1990.)

knocking them down. But still she weaves into the texture of her novel doubts about Namibia as a progressive modern nation.

"Fate" is that which has been predestined. Be has been told that she belongs to a "dying race." By whom was this destiny predicted? By those of her clan? By a stranger? To understand why Be is convinced that death is her "fate," it is necessary to get to the source where it all began,

As a writer, Beake understands that the European language (English in this case) defines the placement of the work of fiction as well as its author, because language is central. The Caucasian writer is always conscious that literature is not merely about individuals, nor are readers isolated members of society. They are representatives of social groups, and the author reflects and extends the spiritual, intellectual, and ethical life of his/her readers. If it is true that for the sake of the Western reader, the Western writer makes a conscious effort to reflect and extend, then we must ask why this effort is not apparent in *Song of Be*. Is it because the Bushman* does not constitute the potential reader-audience? Is it because the writer need not make the same conscious effort for European and American audiences?

Both questions compel one to think about values. How does the writer value the people she is writing about? What is the writer's general concept (notion) of the people whose oral tradition, social structure, ideology, and religion she has not adequately grasped—a people whose traditional culture has been denigrated for centuries, the people themselves relegated by Westerners to subhuman status? The Bushmen in Beake's portraits are like walking corpses, a people for whom place, time, wealth, security, and even life itself hold no purpose. Yet once upon a time the Bushmen were a receptive, loyal people who kept an open door (an open heart) for strangers—for Westerners like those who populate this novel.

The style that Beake has used for her narrative is very similar to that used by Okot p'Bitek in *Song of Lawino*. In *Song of Be* as in *Song of Lawino* both central characters are women, but Lawino is proud of being who she is: a true traditional African woman—a princess who is properly wooed in the African tradition and married into the customs. Come Independence, her once-beloved husband drops her for an African woman who is an imitation of everything foreign. However, even if foreign intervention overwhelmed all else in the country, it did not kill the will of Lawino (the people) to fight the aggressor and live on. In this novel an African

"Bushman" is the preferred designation among those in this ethnic group.

author shares the traditional culture, language, social structure, ideology and religious beliefs of the people. But in *Song of Be* the characters have no identity; they have been displaced, and as Be's grandfather later reveals, he became "insurance" for the son of the stranger who deprived him of his right to live as a man, a human being in his own land. Long before Be came into the world, her maternal grandfather had become an anachronism, an object, an "insurance policy."

Grandfather had been kidnapped with three companions in his youth and brought to the Afrikaner farm as virtually a slave laborer (although such kidnappings were illegal). In trying to escape, one youth had been shot, one died of a broken spirit, and Grandfather had escaped but had returned of his own free will. Finding life in a colonial government town intolerable, he had chosen the farm and the job of tracking elephants for his European boss. He was the keeper of the secretly stashed ivory tusks, which would bail out his boss's heir when economic times were tough.

Beake's characterization of Grandfather as one giving dedicated service in an inhumane system is a throwback to the conventions of early colonialist novels. The character resembles the "contented slave" stereotype.

Be's mother, Aia, has forgotten how to love and will not allow herself to be loved. She believes she had loved Be's father too much, that his drunkenness, infidelity, and violent death were things she could not forget. What this means is that Aia has forgotten that according to most African social traditions, a woman had her own sphere of activity, her own norms, customs, etc. These could be modified depending on her position in the traditional social hierarchy. But her position could in no case be deemed inferior or slavish or even secondary in comparison to the position of a man. But the colonizer's economic demands removed from home the males who were central to the family. For months and years they often worked on farms and in mines, where the only pleasure after work was getting drunk. As foreign influence spread into the hinterland, the lines of traditional male and female lives, which had always moved in a parallel fashion, were eroded. And all the ensuing desolation was at odds with the African concept of life. Emptiness was foreign to Africa for there was always someone there—real or imaginary. But that was of the long ago past. For Be there was no one! Nothing! Her father had succumbed to drink; her mother to a paralyzing disillusionment; her grandfather to dehumanization, to being the keeper of a stockpile of ivory.

Be tells us that she loved Min, the European boss's wife. Min has taught her to read and supplied books from the regional library. But Be is also regularly insulted by Min's frequent references to Bushmen as a "dying race" and her insistence upon using a geography book that treats Be's people as specimens. ("Males of the species are short of stature, usually about five feet tall, and females are shorter and broader because they store more fat.... [They are] distinguished by apricot-colored skin and peppercorn hair" [83]). Moreover, Be displays an irrational trust in Min even at the expense of trust in her own mother. Min suggests that Aia is her husband's mistress, and Be accepts this hint without even questioning her mother.

This bleak array of characterizations is not sufficiently counter-balanced by the author's use of a minor character, Khu, an election-day worker and Be's potential love interest. Khu serves as Beake's political mouthpiece:

> It's no use trying to go back, back in time, back to an old life that doesn't—that can't exist anymore. ... Oh, Be! What times there are ahead for us! The best of times. For too long now we have been speaking as people who do not believe in themselves [92].

Why is this young Bushman portrayed as self-denigrating? Why has Be pricked herself with what she believes to be a poisoned arrow? Why does Be remark about a passing snake: "'I saw a snake just now, a cobra. It looked at me and I looked at it, and then it passed on into the grass as if it had never been there, its smooth coils rippling away from me. Leaving me'" (70). Is her preoccupation with death so unshakeable that she sees herself as an obsolete entity even to a cobra?

"I have just killed myself," because ...
    ... I have lost the will and courage to go on living?
    ... I cannot stand up and fight for what is right and what is mine?
    ... I have been condemned by Western transgressors?

Because? Because? "I have just killed myself" is a way of speaking in riddles that Beake has not yet uncovered herself. But if Bushman history could tell us just one fact, it would be this: that the life-threatening problems of this people have not been self-inflicted.

Be's Admirers

Book critics have had nothing but praise for *Song of Be*, and they are on about the same plane as Beake in their assessment of Namibians as near-prehistoric. Instead of the usual description of modern societies as rural or urban, the *School Library Journal* reviewer refers to Namibians as belonging to a "hunter/gatherer culture" (a euphemism for "primitive," an allusion to people living in disorganized bands) (Andrews, 236). The setting for the novel is 1989, the year preceding formal Namibian independence in 1990. The realities of social/political life have included the long struggle against South Africa's occupation of the area, a struggle dating from the end of World War II. The people have been fighting Apartheid and all the oppression implied in that term. Beake is praised in this review for indicating that the Bushmen will "grow again in pride and identity as they work together to reestablish their values" (236).

But history suggests no loss of identity, no need to regain lost "values." The values have been on Southwest Africa's (Namibia's) side all along as the people took their case to the United Nations, as they argued their case before the International Court of Justice (and won the judgment in 1971 that South African occupation was illegal). Namibian identity was not weak when it produced the resistance organization, the South West African Union (SWANU), when SWANU coordinated its actions with SWAPO (the South West African People's Organization), and when both joined with Angolans to put pressure on the world community (Davidson, *Modern*, 165). The quaint description of contemporary Africans as hunter/gatherers says more about the critic than the West Africans.

Yet this description is repeated in Lois Stover's review in *English Journal*. Be's people, says Stover, were "hunter/gatherers, who kept harmony with the land before the twentieth century found them and changed their lives forever" (86). Seeing Africans as *outside time* is essentially a colonial device, a means of implying that they cannot manage the land or their own affairs *in our time*. Stover says as much when she interprets Be's suicide attempt: "Be feels she can no longer cope with the complexities and chaos around her" (86). Why the long struggle for national independence if attaining it makes life so intolerably complex? The assumption, of course, is that Be is apolitical and ahistorical—her "complexities" merely personal.

In *Booklist* Hazel Rochman refers to Be as "caught between two changing worlds," and her grandfather as a man who is essentially without a country. "After being forced into servitude, ... he once tried to return to his people, but he doesn't belong with them either" (Rochman, 689). Namibians, it seems, are not only outside time; they are also aliens within their own communities. This notion of an outcast status serves colonialist ends; it turns the slavemaster into a rescuer. Both author and critic apparently see the grandfather as inevitably homeless, as not "belonging" with other Bushmen; he is, therefore, presumedly suited to life as an exploited plantation laborer. All this results in "a beautiful novel," according to Rochman (689); "a strong and compassionate look at modern Africa," according to the American Library Association's Notable Book Committee (1352). This committee selected *Song of Be* as a "notable book" for 1994; the ALA "Books for Youth" section selected it as a "best black history title" (1080); and the ALA young adult unit selected it as an "ALA Best Book for Young Adults."

Kirkus Reviews called Be a woman in a "vanishing culture." The colonialist historian Sir Reginald Coupland emphasized a similar perspective when he explained that "the heart of Africa was scarcely beating" before the arrival of Europeans (quoted in Davidson, *Search*, 264). The "dying race" myth, as noted above, was what the colonizers presented to Be as the reality of her being. "You come from a proud race, Be. ... A proud, dying race," says Min, the plantation owner's wife (Beake, 23). We are told that this news saddened Be, but it made no real difference to her. "Min," she said, "was my friend from the beginning" (21). The colonized and colonizer, it seems, have no quarrel, and the "vanishing culture" myth is treated by reviewers as valid even as the twentieth century winds down. Moreover, the publisher selected this *Kirkus* quotation for the back cover of its 1995 paperback edition.

This theme of extinction was common in America prior to Emancipation,* and was a means of rationalizing slavery as an institution. The allegedly inferior African was given a reprieve by the care-giving slavemaster. More than a century later, Africa becomes the target of a similar myth in books for the young.

Conclusion

Children deserve something better than the ahistorical myth that African societies are dysfunctional until Whites undertake their renovation. In 1948

*Writing in 1857, George M. Weston stated: "When the white artisans and farmers want the room which the African occupies, they will take it not by rude force, but by gentle and gradual and peaceful processes. The Negro will disappear, ... perhaps by some process of colonization." This will be the "beneficial result," says Weston, of "laws which nature manifests throughout ... the world." In 1860, clergyman Horace Bushnell also noted that "nature" was at work: "why should it grieve us, that a stock thousands of years behind, in the scale of culture, should die with few and still fewer children to succeed, till finally the whole succession remains in the more cultivated race?" (Quoted in Fredrickson, pp. 154–56.)

Father Placide Tempels, a Franciscan missionary, refuted a popular Western attitude by noting that Africans were not "backward" or underdeveloped. Quite the contrary. He wrote: "We thought that we were educating children, 'big children.' ... And then quite suddenly it seemed that we were dealing after all with an adult humanity, conscious of its own wisdom, penetrated by its own universal philosophy" (166). An evolving history is a condition of all peoples, but this reality is clouded by ill-informed fictions—by authors who pass judgment on groups they know only superficially. Clifford and Beake both resided in Africa, but they apparently carried with them preconceptions that needed to be unlearned. Why produce a book about Africa if you are not in the business of letting children learn of African realities?

Father Tempels noted that "more ink has flowed into those evidently magical and all-conjuring words, 'civilizing mission,' than water from the Congo into the sea" (Davidson, *African Awakening*, 166). The flow continues in children's literature. Authors have not yet abandoned the image of so-called "primitive" men and women; they have not yet felt the need to speak (in Father Tempels' words) from "wisdom to wisdom," from "ideal to ideal," from "one conception of the world to another" (166).

Works Cited

Andrews, Loretta Kreider. Rev. of *Song of Be* by Lesley Beake. *School Library Journal* 40:3 (March, 1994): 236.
Beake, Lesley. *Song of Be*. New York: Henry Holt, 1993.
Clifford, Mary Louise. *Bisha of Burundi*. New York: Thomas Y. Crowell, 1973.
_____. *Salah of Sierra Leone*. New York: Thomas Y. Crowell, 1975.
Davidson, Basil. *Modern Africa*. 3d ed. London and New York: Longman, 1994.
_____. *The Search for Africa: A History in the Making*. London: James Currey, 1994.
Fredrickson, George M. *The Black Image in the White Mind: The Debate on Afro-American Character and Destiny, 1817-1914*. New York: Harper & Row, 1971. Reprint, Middletown, Conn.: Wesleyan University Press, 1987.
Heins, Paul. Rev. of *Salah of Sierra Leone*. *Horn Book* 52:1 (February, 1976): 55.
Johnson, Judy. Rev. of *Salah of Sierra Leone*. *School Library Journal* 22:5 (January, 1976): 52.
Kirkus Reviews. Rev. of *Song of Be* by Lesley Beake. (Dec. 1, 1993): 1520.
Little, K. L. "The Poro Society as an Arbiter of Culture." *African Studies* 7:1 (March, 1948): 1-15.
Mohanty, Chandra. "Under Western Eyes: Feminist Scholarship and Colonial Discourse." *Feminist Review* 30 (August, 1988): 61-88.
Munat, Florence. Rev. of *Song of Be* by Lesley Beake. *VOYA* 17:1 (April, 1994): 22.
"Notable Children's Books, 1994." Rev. of *Song of Be* by Lesley Beake. *Booklist* 90:14 (March 15, 1994): 1352.

p'Bitek, Okot. *Song of Lawino*. Lusaka Close: Nairobi: Modern African Library (originally published by East African Publishing House), 1966.

Rochman, Hazel. Rev. of *Song of Be* by Lesley Beake. *Booklist* 90:7 (December 1, 1993): 689.

Stover, Lois. Rev. of *Song of Be* by Lesley Beake. *English Journal* 83:5 (September, 1994): 86.

Tempels, Father Placide. *La Philosophie Bantoue*. (Quoted in Basil Davidson's *The African Awakening*. London: Jonathan Cape, 1955.)

"Year in Black History for Young People." Rev. of *Song of Be* by Lesley Beake. *Booklist* 90:12 (February 15, 1994): 1080.

The Lion Lobbyists

Environmentalism in an African Context

Plush monkeys, plastic hippos, stuffed lions—these are the child's vicarious companions, playthings that prepare the way for encounters with the environmental novel. Similarly, early childhood story hours establish that sympathy with the animal kingdom that novelists work to expand and deepen. In Betty Dinneen's *Lion Yellow* (1975) and Eric Campbell's *The Place of Lions* (1990) the crusade for environmental protection centers on game reserves in Kenya and Tanzania. But the conservation theme in both books is coupled with the assumption that save-the-earth programs must be primarily the domain of Europeans. Dinneen treats Africans as suffering from such a serious time lag that she can conceive of their participation only at some future date. A Western education is the prerequisite. Campbell casts doubt on African competence and integrity, drawing on the minstrel show tradition for his caricatures. The Caucasians have evolved from "great white hunters" into "great white environmentalists."

That the preservation of the planet is important to all its inhabitants is not at issue here. The novels under discussion in this critique are about power over the planet—about control over resources and, consequently, control over the distribution of wealth. "Empire," write Neil Smith and Anne Godlewska, "was ... a quintessentially geographical project" (2). Geography is concerned with the earth's surface—with its conditions and the relationship of those conditions with animal, plant, and human life. More importantly, "geography constitutes the taking of possession of the earth, and the intellectual domination of space" (quoted in Godlewska from *De l'Histoire des Sciences à l'Histoire de la Pensée*, 1977). Students of the history of geography are opting for the thesis that "geography is made in the mind" (Wesso, 317). In particular, they are tracing the history of the imperial idea and finding the roots of the myth that "nature" ordains whites as the masters of the world.

Using two separate children's literature traditions (the family story in *Lion Yellow* and the adventure tale in *The Place of Lions*), Dinneen and Campbell bring reader sympathies into line with a particular interpretation of geographical space. Conservationist ideals are put forward but not without a heavy dose of neocolonialist propaganda. In these novels, to lobby for the lion is to simultaneously cast aspersions on the African people; it is the means by which geographical "truth" becomes synonymous with European sovereignty over Africa. Africa is still up for grabs, only now the environmental "missionary" is on the scene. Christianity and its civilize-the-savage ploy will not work this time around.

Lion Yellow

An engaging "settler" family is juxtaposed with an equally appealing lion group in Dinneen's novel. By shifting from one to the other, the author reinforces the idea that a family is a family whatever the species—that it warrants preservation at all costs. Yet the Wageni and Masai peoples are never seen as part of a positive family environment. The Wageni, we are told, are foolishly laying claim to the animal reserve, intending to convert it into a new grazing area for their herds. They are officially pressing their claim with the Kenyan Ministry of Lands, but the child reader does not learn the specifics of their argument. Instead, the reader hears the pleas of the European environmentalist:

> Ben Thorne [the European game warden] knew that the small game park ... would not long survive if the goats and cattle came. The perfect balance of grazers, browsers, tree-nibblers, meat-eaters and scavengers would be upset. The proportion of grassland to forest was not high. The banks of the pools and stream fed by the springs would be trampled to a barren mudflat by the ever-increasing herds of cattle, ... while the grasslands near the water would become semi-desert. In a few years the Wageni would be no better off, the wild animals would be decimated, and the game park ruined [44–45].

Given his European education, Ben Thorne is allegedly privy to this knowledge of delicate balances. Africans, it seems, have no grasp of African ecology, even though they have preserved this landscape for millions of years. Moreover, their cattle herds are portrayed as if they had no purpose other than being spoilers of God's green earth. David Thorne, the son in the European family, makes this ecstatic proclamation: "Whose land is this? Mine, mine, mine" (102). And to reinforce the point, the novel's narrator restates David's gleeful realization: "'Our land,'" he thought. "'Mine and the lion's'" (102). If anyone has believed that geography was apolitical, this unquestioning sense of possession should arouse second thoughts. David is making a direct claim to ownership, inheritance, and rulership. Using the environmental mask, the white settler and his family are dispossessing Africans of their land and basing this maneuver on the broadly appealing save-the-earth agenda. "Historically," writes Smith and Godlewska, "nothing characterizes geography so tellingly as its close contacts with those either seeking or holding territorial power" (4). Actually, land grabs are no more concerned with environmental protection than genuine Christianity was concerned with baptising people and then selling them into slavery.

The political equation, Europeans over Africans, is implicit in this novel as the story evolves with a cast of African subordinates who work for Mr. Thorne. They are "rangers" who bicycle across the plains and keep track of animal movements and general well-being. They dwell in mud huts at some distance from the warden's house, but the reader sees them primarily in relation to the whites (i.e., doing the cooking, polishing the Land Rover, doing the laundry). One Masai ranger, Thomas, is a favorite of young David and is commended by the author as one of the "most trusted men." In the same sentence the reader learns that "he had moved away from tradition and his father's cattle herds to earn his living as a game ranger" (50). Thomas is introduced as comic relief, telling the Thorne children of his escapade with a new lion in the region:

> "I leave the Springs. I ride here. Everything fine. Then, two miles out, I ride down the hill—near Roaring Rocks. I am happy. I sing to myself. And then he come, *simba* with the black mane, very quick, charging across the grass. Me, I am already racing downhill, very quick. But I go faster! I yell at him, I sing to him the old songs of my people, very fierce. I stand high—so—on the pedals and make my feet fly. And still he come! Ehhhhhhh!" said Thomas, shaking his head. "It very bad ... I threw my cap at him. I think, maybe cap enough. And he think so too.... Better cap than me. I too tough. I hurt his stomach" [52].

Despite this near-fatal experience, the black rangers continue riding on bicycles through the game park, and only the European rides within the safe enclosure of a Land Rover. A policy change is considered only when Thomas takes young David out on a bicycle and they barely escape with their lives.

Only one other African has a pivotal position in the story, Mr. Likimani, who is Minister of Lands and is adjudicating the Wageni land claim.

For the first time we hear about African family life, but the portrait maligns the Masai people while justifying the Europeans. Moreover, the portrait is in Mr. Likimani's own words; he is given the task of narrating the story of his abused childhood, even his rejection at the hands of his parents:

> ... when I was still a child I fell and broke my leg.... It was the time of the rains, and it was some months before my father was able to carry me to a mission hospital, a hundred miles away. There they cared for me, and later educated me. For when my father saw that I did not grow tall and strong like my brothers, and could not run and jump with the other boys, he did not consider me good enough to rejoin my family and tribe [137].

The government minister then gloats over the fact that he can read and write, and the family members who rejected him are considered to be "primitives." "'That,'" says Likimani, "'is what is called irony, is it not?'" (137).

Having been schooled in England as the protege of the missionaries, Mr. Likimani is portrayed as someone receptive to Western influences, but still the outcome of the Wageni/Thorne dispute remains in question. Only after the minister experiences a personal epiphany in the company of a white child does he come through for the environmentalist cause. The author builds a special bond between this African adult, a European child, and a cub-rearing lioness. When the youngest in the Thorne family, Robin, comes suddenly upon the lioness, Mr. Likimani edges his way toward the beast and stares it down. The little girl is safe and the Masai has, for the first time in his life, achieved a state of manhood in Masai terms. (Or so we are told.) There is now a "glint in his eye"; the game warden comments: "He looks as if someone's given him a present" (143).

To emphasize the importance of this transformation, the author has Mr. Likimani bestow his father's shield upon young David—a shield scored with the marks of lion claws. "I have always kept it to remind me of the side of my people's life I missed. But I don't think I need it any more" (144). Assimilation, it seems, has finally caught up with him. Giving away the shield is symbolic of giving away the land of the Wageni without first giving them a chance to prove their claim. Likimani is part of the assimilado clique, the Western-educated neocolonialists who would readily mortgage Africa because they do not believe in themselves or their people. An eight-year-old European has been the means of the Government Minister's self-respect (and his newly-gained conviction that the

Thornes should keep "their" game reserve). All this is interpreted as a feat of real courage. The minister speaks of the "courage to face your lions, wherever you meet them" (144). The Wageni land claim is just a "lion" that the Minister has learned to stare down.

Dinneen wrote this novel fifteen years after the declaration of Kenyan independence, yet this event is treated as a mere *pro forma* happening. It apparently has no meaningful consequences for the African work force. Mr. Thorne tells his children that eventually the "Europeans will have to move over" since Kenya now has independence and an African game warden could conceivably be hired. But the children are not to worry. Since Robin brought the minister face to face with a lion, the immediate future is safe for Europeans (and, by extension, for the endangered animal kingdom). According to Mr. Thorne, "'There's bound to be more greedy eyes cast on the parks, but this time I think we've made it'" (143). This is neo-colonialism in a nutshell: greed is allegedly the impulse behind "Africa for the Africans," whereas "Africa for the Europeans" represents pure altruism.

To make this anomaly credible Dinneen positions African characters in subservient roles or elevates them solely by means of European education, philanthropy, and contact. Then she indicates that only an infinitesimal number of Africans have been sufficiently westernized to allow true self-determination in Kenya to succeed. Moreover, premature authority in African hands would mean the devastation of the delicate African ecosystem, and the world as a whole would be the loser. What better way to implant this message in young minds than through dramatizing warm family relationships in the European and lion worlds? This double "family" chronicle, however, leaves the African family obscure and marginalized.

Lion Identity, African Invisibility

The families of the African park rangers receive almost no mention in this novel. When young David is agonizing over his prospects ("What'll we do if we lose the game park? Where would we go?"), what do we hear of the concerns of the African children? Have these children any right to live in the land of their ancestors? Have their parents any authority in planning for their future? And when David and Robin are doing correspondence-course lessons with their mother and sending term papers to teachers in Nairobi, what educational system is in place for the African children? Do we see any makeshift classrooms for the rangers' youngsters? When the Thorne children go for an outing on the beach of the Indian Ocean or have a shopping spree in Nairobi, do we see the African children treated to a picnic on game park profits? Do the African and white children have any contact with one another as friends and playmates? No. Although the ranger called Thomas is treated as a friend to David and Robin, the alleged risk in such a relationship comes out eventually. That is, when Thomas and David ride off on bicycles to scare off Prince (a competing male lion), Mr. Thorne's anger is voiced in racist terms: "Haven't you any brains at all? I know Thomas is a madman when it comes to lions. But if a boy with your upbringing doesn't know you don't fool with lions, who should?" (162). The character of even the most "trusted" African is called in question here, while the rights of Africans are circumvented throughout.

Dinneen invites the reader to empathize with the Thorne family and to consider them the God-sent protectors of animals. The young audience is not to consider the unseen families of rangers, servants, or Wageni herders.

Lion family life, on the other hand, is minutely described. Soldani (father lion) and his many wives (Meriam, Fawzia, Elder Sister, The Lady, etc.) share a culture and a community that is depicted with great sympathy and charm. We learn about their instincts, moods, attitudes, protective mechanisms, eating patterns, and more. When Prince, another male, challenges Soldani, the reader becomes a spectator to their confrontations. But no such witnessing transpires vis-à-vis the Thorne/ Wageni dispute. We listen in on the discussions between Mr. Thorne and the Minister of Lands, but the Wagenis and their relationship to their claim is never known. As Ben Thorne and Soldani are both leaders and protectors of their families, so Thorne is allowed to take full charge and be the spokesperson for the Wagenis. He obviously discredits their position, highlights the position of the animals, and achieves his own purpose (which means claiming Africa as his permanent and rightful home).

And not even the story of the animals is accurately told. In truth, the Kenyan people lived with and among wild animals for eons. They did not hunt them down for trophies or make a business of selling skins and ivory. While greed exists everywhere, it did not cause the devastation of the African landscape prior to the European incursion.

This whole scenario about animal preservation versus indigenous land use lines up quite explicitly with the goals of empire education as it was formulated in the late nineteenth century in Great Britain. The geography curriculum was designed to impress people in the colonies with the central position of England—its unchallengeable place at the center of the world economy. And concurrently, the people who remained in Great Britain were to learn about the glories of the colonies. To carry forward this agenda, Oxford University established the Geographical Association and its publication, *The Geographical Teacher*. And teachers were not only encouraged to use this resource; in Cape Province, the Education Department subsidized the teacher's subscription fees (Wesso, 319).

Politics, land use, economics, teacher education, children—they are all bound together in the geographic enterprise. Jonathan Crush, in a study of this social/political mix in South Africa, states the case concisely: "...imperialism itself was an act of geographic violence through which space was explored, reconstructed, re-named and controlled" (337).

The Place of Lions

Like Dinneen, Eric Campbell uses the juxtaposition of English and lion families, but his novel is essentially in the adventure mode. He gets rid of immediate human family members through death (the mother) and through an airplane crash that disables the father. Now the teenage protagonist, Chris Harris, must use his own inner resources for survival on the Serengeti Plain. But young Chris is not left without an adult role model. Mike Taylor, a white tour guide and former warden in a Tanzanian game reserve, is running down poachers while simultaneously taking a rich American on a safari to photograph elephants. He is a rough and rugged conservationist who has resigned in disgust over the Tanzanian government's mismanagement of wildlife. His sidekick is his African driver (Bennie), a servant who grins incessantly while obeying commands and being bribed with a little hard cash.

No other Africans appear in the novel except the despicable poachers (who are Somalis) and the taxi drivers covering the airport-hotel route. The poachers are predictable villains, their cruelties expected. But by associating the ivory market with blacks rather than whites, Campbell turns history on its head. Clearly those who came for ivory, furs, and exotic trophies for their walls were outsiders. But with this novel the European and Euro-American child need have no pangs of environmental guilt.

Additionally, Campbell develops a layer of "entertainment" for non-Africans by turning black taxi drivers into modern-day minstrel performers. These clowns are alternately happy-go-lucky and churlish. They serve the narrative as comic relief, but they are unmistakably dangerous—a population that would in all likelihood mess up a wildlife refuge or any constructive phenomenon that came their way. The poachers send one kind of anti-African message and the general work force another. A colonialist apologia is the result.

Kilimanjaro airport was teeming with taxis—that is, with "an amazing assortment of junkyard vehicles with windshields missing, odd wheels, wrong hoods, bald tires" (19–20). On landing, Chris and his father are "instantly surrounded and deafened" by "ragged taxi drivers [who] grabbed their bags out of their hands, tugged their shirts, pushed, guided, jostled, and cajoled" them (19). In a cross between "blackface" and "Tarzan" theatricality, one driver breaks through the din of "whooping and jeering" drivers who are literally exchanging blows over the chance to serve the travelers. "'Me, bwana. This way, bwana… You're lucky. These people are snakes. They will cheat you. I, Josephu, do not cheat'" (20–21). This driver "gave an ear-piercing whoop, and hurled himself back into the melee" to retrieve the luggage. Then in a vehicle with only a third and fourth gear and no clutch, the travelers are pushed onto the airport exit road by the whole company of drivers. "Whooping with joy," Josephu steers the car at seventy miles an hour in front of a huge semi truck. "The tires screamed in fury, and the car threatened to turn onto its side as both passenger-side wheels came off the ground" (23). And so it goes as this six-page, minstrel-like sketch introduces the reader to Africa, to an alternately grinning and wrangling corps of blue-collar workers.

Children's books about Africa frequently perpetuate the myth that Africans cannot learn about or handle machinery, and Campbell misses no opportunity to emphasize this notion. Besides the scenes with the "junkyard" taxis, we have general descriptions of Tanzania: "buses broke down and stayed that way; the towns and the roads were collapsing; electricity failed regularly; water came through the taps only spasmodically; and gasoline had been rationed for months" (26). This last item is usually obtained through "wheeling and dealing on the black market and some well-placed bribes."

Bribes are only one example of corruption. Bennie, the tour-bus driver, boasts that he can terrorize tourists at will and not be arrested because "the police chief is my uncle" (27). (The driver has placed a snake in a tourist's camera bag as a joke.) In conversation with his safari customer, Mike explains about Tanzanians in general:

> Unless you watch their every move [the movements of Africans who repair cars] they steal your good inner tubes and replace them with worn-out, perished junk with about a hundred patches in already. They should send budding magicians to this country. What Tanzanians don't know about sleight of hand isn't worth knowing. They can pick your pockets without coming within twenty feet of you [140].

If Tanzanians are this abominable, why do people like Mike Taylor stay on? Why must a save-the-earth propaganda piece be so abusive of Africans and their government? What kind of life does Mr. Harris want for his son if he decides to reside in a country where the people are rogues and reprobates from top to bottom? How can Chris, who became a misfit following the death of his mother, fit into a new society when his attitude toward it is so negative?

But if Tanzanians are dishonorable and base, the Somalis are much more contemptible. Their infamy includes the slaughter of animals, and that makes them more abominable than their East African neighbors. Even the gruff American tourist is shocked by the great elephant carcasses, by the "terrible holes of blood where the tusks had been axed out of their skulls" (97). "'I seen animals killed before,'" he says. "'And I ain't no animal rights nut, nor nothing like that. But somehow—I can't explain it too well—somehow, there's fair and there's not fair'" (142). If this largely illiterate American is stirred with emotion, then the carnage must be terrible indeed.

The Somalis do not only slaughter beasts, they become the stereotypic "black brute" as delineated by Campbell. The danger faced by the young hero is played to the hilt:

> Towering over him was a hugh black man ... in his hands the gun that had just jabbed Chris in the back. ... He grinned ... contemptuously, revealing blackened teeth filed to sharp points. The savage strangeness of his mouth heightened Chris's fear. ... The man's lips curled back over his filed teeth. His grin had gone and taking its place was a sneer of such savagery, such viciousness, that a huge wave of fear rose up from Chris's stomach [160, 167].

Given this portrait, we can easily empathize with Chris's anxiety. Moreover, the African "brute" becomes all the more horrific when made to play a role-reversing part with the fearsome lion. While Chris is stalked by the human "brute," the lion serves as companion and protector:

> Chris studied the [lion]. He had stopped licking his leg and was sitting back, doglike, presenting a massive, bony profile. ... They rose together up the side of the hill, the boy first, the great, slow figure, like a huge, faithful, golden dog, a few feet behind. Two spirits caught and held. Bound in a magic, brief but eternal [177, 191].

The author jumps back and forth from the aging lion story, to the subplot about ivory poaching, to the injured teenage protagonist and his lonely quest to find aid for his disabled father. Then Campbell brings the different story strands together: the poachers first abandon Chris and then try to kidnap him; one of them is killed by the "doglike" lion; the threesome on safari see the lion with Chris but refrain from shooting it because boy and lion have clearly developed an unfathomable bond. Instinct communicates this to Mike Taylor before he rushes in with his rifle. By contriving this element of fantasy, the author accentuates the idea that animals and humans are not warring entities. On the contrary, Chris has seen Africa and has "come to terms with its savagery and nobility" (194). But it is the lions that express nobility, while the Africans are portrayed as subservient, ridiculous, cruel, and lawless.

Joining the cause of environmentalism with stereotypes of Africans has a certain negative "logic" in the 1990s, a decade in which environmental concerns are on the rise while race relations plummet. The juxtaposition has occurred before, especially following the first World War when horses died miserably and unattended on the battlefields of France. Hugh Lofting, a member of the "Irish Guards" and a witness to this tragedy, conceived "Doctor Dolittle" as the ultimate animal protector. But racism was also rampant in the post-war years, and Lofting's *Story of Doctor Dolittle* (1920) has since been recognized by some professionals as a prime example of racist indoctrination.*

But while the environmentalism-racism linkage has been exposed by a few children's book critics (especially by Isabelle Suhl in *Interracial Books for Children Bulletin*, vol. 2: 1 and 2, 1969), the essence of that connection remains as the twentieth century winds down. The context of the

---

*In The Story of Doctor Dolittle *and its sequels, the Doctor symbolizes the conservationist cause with his strategies to sabotage fox hunts, bull fights, badly managed circuses, etc. His African characters are a blend of self-hate, irrationality, and cannibalistic violence.

Campbell novel in the 1990s is what we could call "environmental imperialism."

Environmental Imperialism

Environmentalist fiction for children is an expanding field, and, generally speaking, a positive one. But for some reason authors fail too often to recount the truly astounding history of animal decimation—the stories of hunting parties by colonial lords and their slaughter of a hundred lions in one day! Also a problem arises in works that shift the blame from Western over-consumption and age-old pollution to the peoples of Africa and elsewhere in the so-called "third world." Addressing conservationism and its present political ramifications, historian Thomas Spear points out that "we blame Africans for not conserving their wildlife, when the establishment of game parks has threatened both domestic herds and wildlife by artificially constricting their grazing routines" (18). This development is purely for the sake of wealthy Western tourists. Similarly,

> We blame Brazilians for callously destroying the tropical rain forest, heedless of the needs of ... rubber tappers and landless peasants for its resources or of the fact that it is our pollution and destruction of our own forests that makes preservation of their rain forest so critical [Spear, 18].

The problem is not, however, merely one of newly-found hindsight on the part of Westerners, or a desire to avoid a continuing deterioration of the planet. Americans alone consume over half of the earth's resources while constituting only 5 percent of the world's population. A person in the United States, says Spear, consumes "hundreds of times the resources of an African." This makes the depletion of the planet a largely Western phenomenon.

Blaming the victim is a familiar tactic of white supremacists, and this strategy can be traced within the context of colonialism. According to Spear, colonialism is a self-justifying ideology. European colonialism required that Europeans "conquer and exploit others for the others' benefit," and at the same time deny "the benefits colonialists themselves received from colonial exploitation" (18). Environmentalism is arguably a new "civilizing mission," a new imperialism, a new self-serving morality. Spear advises that "to improve the world's environment, we [in the

West] must be prepared both to reduce our own consumption and to share our remaining wealth."

Ironically, Africa is in the position of being not only a locale for conservationist crusades but also a proposed locale for the dumping of toxic wastes. In a 1992 memo by World Bank economist Larry Summers, a suggestion for "dirty industries" was made as follows: "Shouldn't the World Bank be encouraging more migration of the dirty industries to the LDCS [Lesser Developed Countries]?" (Rich, 247). Environmentalist children's novels prompt the curious mind to ask who is bringing this story about planet safety and high finance to a young readership.

Conclusion

The planet's present crisis is a timely subject for writers who gear their works toward the young, but so far a balanced discussion—one that examines both Western and "third world" involvement—has not been forthcoming. This issue is not likely to surface as an important one in children's book circles since the work of Eric Campbell is perceived as an excellent model. Steven Engelfried, writing for *The School Library Journal*, noted: "Overall, the exciting action in a fascinating setting, coupled with the intriguing spiritual element, make this a worthwhile and thought-provoking book" (117). And more important, the American Library Association's notable book committee selected *The Place of Lions* for inclusion in its list of "Best Books for Young Adults, 1993." This honor is based on the book's "proven or potential appeal and value to young adults" (1340).

Do children's book professionals in the West really share Mr. Campbell's disapproving views of Africans? Apparently they do, even though they are probably like the young hero, Chris Harris, who has not even had a chance to know them.

To facilitate a land grab, says historian George M. Fredrickson, a doctrine is necessary. "A mode of thinking … helped set the parameters...." (7). Writing about South Africa, Fredrickson notes that "[the European] invaders did not confront the native peoples without certain preconceptions about their nature that helped shape the way they pursued their goals" (7). Concepts about "savagery" were one part of the distorting lens.

The lens that is at work in children's books connects with the way sociopolitical goals are being pursued. This truism cannot be overlooked when we address environmentalism.

Works Cited

"Best Books for Young Adults, 1993." *Booklist* 89:14 (March 15, 1993): 1342.

Campbell, Eric. *The Place of Lions*. London: Macmillan Children's Books, 1990; San Diego: Harcourt Brace, 1991.

Crush, Jonathan. "Post-colonialism, De-colonialism, and Geography." In *Geography and Empire*. Ed. Anne Godlewska and Neil Smith. Oxford, England, and Cambridge, Mass.: Blackwell, 1994; pp. 334–50.

Dinneen, Betty. *Lion Yellow*. Illustrated by Charles Robinson. New York: Walck, 1975.

Englefried, Steven. Rev. of *The Place of Lions* by Eric Campbell. *School Library Journal* 37:11 (November, 1991): 116–17.

Fredrickson, George M. *White Supremacy: A Comparative Study in American and South African History*. New York & Oxford: Oxford University Press, 1981.

Godlewska, Anne, and Neil Smith, eds. *Geography and Empire*. Oxford, England, and Cambridge, Mass.: Blackwell, 1994.

Rich, Bruce. *Mortgaging the Earth: The World Bank, Environmental Impoverishment, and the Crisis of Development*. Boston: Beacon Press, 1994.

Smith, Neil, and Anne Godlewska. "Introduction: Critical Histories of Geography." In *Geography and Empire*. Ed. Anne Godlewska and Neil Smith. Oxford, England, and Cambridge, Mass.: Blackwell, 1994; pp. 1–8.

Spear, Thomas. "The Environment: White Man's Burden." *Christian Science Monitor* (November 30, 1990): 18.

Wesso, Harold. "The Colonization of Geographic Thought: The South African Experience." In *Geography and Empire*. Ed. Anne Godlewska and Neil Smith. Oxford, England, and Cambridge, Mass.: Blackwell, 1994.

Neocolonialist Comedy

Literary and Pictorial Stereotyping
in Do You Know Me

Nancy Farmer's *Do You Know Me* (1993) features an eventful, farcical adjustment from life in war-torn Mozambique to life in peaceful Zimbabwe. But what Farmer actually presents is a Negrophobic piece of many dimensions. The novel cannot be described as a story based on anything that resembles truthful characterization, especially with regard to the protagonist, Uncle Zeka.

As the starring "comic," Uncle Zeka moves from one demonstration of maladjustment to another, while his young niece, Tapiwa, looks on admiringly. Throughout the book, real communication stops at one level: the nine-year-old Tapiwa conferring and associating with her middle-aged uncle. The author brings home to her readers one obsessive message, one central image of African people as symbolized by a man with the mind of a nine-year-old. Uncle Zeka communicates with and is understood by no character in the novel except his young niece; and once this point is made, the author has confirmed the centuries-old belief of Westerners—namely, that African minds develop no further than the minds of children.

In the subplot we meet another family, Tapiwa's Aunt Rudo and Uncle Soso, the latter being Zimbabwe's Minister of Progress. With this couple the author mocks the elitist pretensions that supposedly infect the minds of African government officials. We have met such stereotypes before, especially in the plantation narratives of the American south after the Civil War. While Farmer uses an independent African country as her setting, this tale could have been situated in any of the southern states of the U.S. during the last century. It would seem that since portrayals of American blacks have changed somewhat, an independent African country becomes the convenient venue for confirming old stereotypes. Farmer's characters are not different from the rural plantation "Sambo"

(Uncle Zeka) and the urban dandy "Tambo" (Aunt Rudo and spouse). The simple bush people are "primitives"—people locked in a backward condition both physically and mentally. The Minister of Progress and his friends parade about in classy clothes, expensive cars, and all the trappings of the "assimilados" (Africans imitating all the wrong things in Western culture). The "blackface" minstrel shows of the 19th century proclaimed the same basic message about ex-slave fools and pretenders.

Why does Farmer pursue the same Western duplicity that characterized the nineteenth century and carry its propaganda to the fourth-to-sixth graders of today? Why is she taking children back to a period in history known for portraying African-American blacks as absurd and subhuman? This revival of tarnished and distorted images from the past carries with it many painful scars; it does not make for a healthy climb toward interracial harmony in the twenty-first century. The details of the novel's plot and characterizations—the particulars of the Negrophobic story—only make these questions more perplexing. Moreover, book critics have taken Farmer's side, a subject we will explore shortly.

What Makes a Story Negrophobic?

Before we examine plot and character, it is worth stating that humor is not a feature that can come to this book's defense. Comedy is a phenomenon that reaffirms social bonds. Sociologist Hugh Dalziel Duncan writes:

> Comedy teaches us that men [and women] can endure much if they can endure it in rational discourse with each other. When we cannot communicate in reason we are ready for the tortured image of tragedy. We do not laugh at the fearful monsters of the dream. But we laugh at any danger, even death itself, so long as we laugh together [403–4].

He adds that joy is always the shared joy of one "who is laughed at, as well as [one] who laughs." But "when laughter passes into derision, mockery, and the grotesque, it is no longer comic" (404). In Farmer's book there is no "communication in reason"; there is only derision and the misunderstanding of a people's culture.

On our first meeting with Uncle Zeka, we are told he has traveled on foot through the bush from Mozambique, that he has lost his life savings (a cache of gold nuggets) to bandits, and that his home has been reduced to ashes. This story holds great fascination for nine-year-old

Tapiwa, and the little girl follows her uncle everywhere. However, she keeps her distance, perhaps because this has become a reflex action as she evades taunting remarks from snobbish schoolmates. In any case, like any African elder, Uncle Zeka is perfectly aware of his niece's presence and in due time remarks: "My shadow follows me everywhere." As she discreetly follows him, he discreetly communicates their special friendship and bonding. Unfortunately, this positive relationship is not allowed to grow in a positive direction. Farmer does not establish for Western readers any knowledge of how young African children are educated culturally by their elders. Instead, the author manipulates two sets of characters: the despicable assimilados (Aunt Rudo and husband) and Zeka-the-peasant.

In making this contrast, the author suggests the idea that well-off blacks detest their own kith and kin. Additionally, the reader sees how Aunt Rudo and Minister Soso mistreat their African servants. In conveying the abusive treatment of relatives, a situation is created by the author whereby Uncle Zeka, Tapiwa, and her brother, Tongai, are taken to live with Aunt Rudo and Uncle Soso while the children's mother is hospitalized. The residence is no doubt one of the colonial buildings constructed by the whites who did not anticipate political change. "The house was two stories high and had at least fifteen bedrooms. Marble stairs led up to the front door. All the windows had decorative ironwork on the outside, which Tapiwa thought was pretty until she realized it was also like the bars on a prison" (67). To keep out African burglars, the surrounding walls were trimmed with broken glass, a live electric wire was stretched above the glass, and a peek-hole in the gate allowed the gardener to check on any visitors.

Uncle Zeka is installed in the Kaya, the servants' houses at the far end of the garden. These are shacks with rusty iron roofs, smoke-blackened walls, a single faucet for bathing, and a hole-in-the-ground "bathroom." Maids, cooks, gardeners, and chauffeur live here without heat or electricity. Tapiwa is told to take no food from the refrigerator and to stay away from the mangoes. The sugar is "kept in a metal box with a padlock on it" (81), but Aunt Rudo meets at the best restaurants with her friends (all members of the War on Hunger Ladies Club). The contrast between Uncle Soso's stinginess and his vision of progress is underscored by his boasts: "'Did you know [that] if you lined up the bricks [of the hospital wing] end to end, they would reach all the way to Nairobi? They use ten thousand four hundred eighty cotton swabs every week and eight hundred gallons of rubbing alcohol" (70). By depicting this official and his wife as self-serving, wasteful, hypocritical, and mean-spirited, the author reaffirms the stale motif about mismanagement of wealth. In a word, we hear the well-worn colonialist message: "It is not time for change!" "The *people* will never change!" "As it was in the beginning, so will it ever be!" "Without whites, Africa is doomed!"

Farmer's portrait of country folk is even more damaging, as well as more conclusive, in its implied statement about the need for "White Saviors." Uncle Zeka's experiments with traps and foods end in near-disasters, although his motive is understandable (i.e., he is trying to pay his own way as he resides in his brother's household). His childishness and apparent intellectual backwardness make one wonder how he could have lasted a week in the bush. His behavior is that of the minstrel clown rather than that of the unschooled villager. For example, he concocts a caterpillar stew without first learning that urban caterpillars are toxic. He ends up in the emergency room of the hospital with a stomach full of poison. When he decides to harvest a mice crop, he sets fire to a vacant lot between two houses. The children's warnings are brushed aside with the blithe comment: "Grass burns so fast it will be out before you know it" (16). He does not test the direction of the wind or consider that the "fierce crackling flames" are being driven straight toward his niece and nephew (whom he has positioned at the end of the lot to wallop fleeing mice). And so it goes with one chaotic scheme after another. Apparently it is believed that the child reader will be excited by Uncle's bravado and violation of rules.

But again and again it is clear that Zeka's storehouse of knowledge is too incomplete to be functional. He traps bees in one of his hand-woven baskets, but loses control when he lets them loose. In explaining that swarming bees cannot sting, he tells his niece: "You city people don't know anything about the bush," but it is clear from the havoc he creates that *he* doesn't know anything about it either (59). That is, his slim supply of facts will not bring him to the fulfillment of his well-intentioned plans, and this translates into great discomfort for others:

> The humming [of the bees] rose almost to a shriek… [Tapiwa] ran into the reeds, cutting herself on their sharp leaves. She didn't care. Gasping with terror, she tore through the marsh until she reached the pond and threw herself in. The bottom was slimy, and for an instant she thought her feet were stuck in the mud, but she managed to drag them free. She crouched in the ooze with her head under the water [62].

Luckily Uncle Zeka has already taught her that a reed can become a breathing tube. But although she keeps alive with such a reed, numerous bee stingers are implanted in her head and she is one sick kid by the time her father rescues her. Uncle Zeka develops a fever as the result of his multiple stings and takes to his bed. His poor judgment and half-baked "bush" expertise are one part of this episode. Another part relates to Zeka's theft of railway ties as kindling for his fire. He promises to discontinue such pilfering but only because the ties "don't burn at all well" (61). His rationalizations about railroad lines are infantile at best: "Look at the railroad tracks. They only need enough to keep the rails apart. The bits sticking out at the side are wasted" (58). In any case, Zeka steals a whole wooden tie for his fire (64) and is unable to foresee the danger this imposes on rail passengers.

In another debacle with machines, he again risks the life of his niece—he drives a Mercedes Benz at breakneck speed into an abandoned mine shaft. Prior to the crash, Zeka uses his childish mentality as he explains to Tapiwa the art of driving:

> "The way to know when to change *gears*" said Uncle Zeka, "is when the car begins to cry." ... Uncle Zeka went faster until a piercing noise came from the motor. "There! The car is crying. It is saying, 'Give me another *gear*.' ... Cars are like donkeys. If they don't want to pull the car, they try to kick you" [83-84].

When Tapiwa urges her uncle to stop driving in the middle of the road, he replies: "That's the best way. ... You won't run into trees and so forth" (84). On hills he turns off the motor in order to save money and then comments gleefully, "if the hill is really steep, you can go as fast as a racing car" (86). Zeka has had driving lessons from Aunt Rudo's chauffeur, but his mind is such that his only means of comprehension is to translate machines into animals. He roars down an incline, fails to negotiate a turn, and sends himself and two passengers into an abandoned gold mine.*

His citified relatives are alternately exasperated and sympathetic, but

---

*Uncle Zeka resembles Joel Chandler Harris' Uncle Remus in these slapstick encounters with mechanical objects. Harris creates sketches in which the ex-slave blunders his way through the post-Reconstruction era in a state of fright and/or disbelief over such gadgets as the telephone and the phonograph. When his employer, Miss Sally, explains the phonograph's wax cylinder, the old man is incredulous: "...how dat ar brass ban' gwine git in dar... My mid' pi'ntedly tells me dat ef [de big horn, bass drum, etc.] wuz all ter git in dat ar shebang dar, dey'd bust it wide open." See Uncle Remus and His Friends (Boston: Houghton Mifflin, 1892).

the whole set-up lacks credibility. Zeka was attacked by a crocodile in boyhood, but his brother has no apparent knowledge of this, as evidenced by his attempt to get Zeka a boating job. It seems that Zeka's phobia about water is not part of family lore, despite the huge scar that remains on his leg. Has Zeka had no contact with his family? Has there been an unbridgeable chasm between country and city family members? To plant such an idea in a story about Europeans or Euro-Americans would result in charges of implausibility, but in behavioral terms Farmer puts Africans on a different planet and hears no complaints. As in many Negrophobic-Darwinian stories, the characterization of Zeka makes him more child than adult. He suffers from arrested development; he is seen to have little capacity to deal with abstractions, to compare, analyze, predict, hypothesize, infer, deduce, or reason beyond what the concrete conditions of the moment suggest to him. This is one of many signs of Negrophobia in this text. But book reviewers have seen only humor, love, and most bewilderingly, cultural pluralism.

Critical Accolades and Cultural Errors

The reviewer for *Publishers Weekly* calls this novel a "most interesting window on a culture" (89). In *Booklist*, Janice Del Negro recommends this title "for libraries interested in cultural plurality" (1431). By failing to recognize an outdated colonial story, such critics join Farmer in destroying what has been so assiduously won by good-intentioned writers and educators, both black and white.

    Cultural confusions often stem from a Western slant imposed on situations, and since critics share Farmer's general orientation, they fail to notice. Lyn Miller-Lachman notes that one positive outcome of the plot action is that "other family members ... learn humility and understanding as they come to terms with their village relative" (118). This observation is jarring to those who understand the strong communal bonds that are typically created and sustained. Africans do not "come to terms" with their village relations. Relations are relations, period. Ever present in the traditional African psyche is the importance of humility and mutual understanding. These values are to be practiced vis-à-vis community and noncommunity members, as well as parents and village elders. African ethics, norms, and behavioral patterns have been misused and misunderstood by Westerners—by observers who have never tried to comprehend the meaning of religious, community, and domestic life practices.

In looking for recognizable cultural elements, Lois F. Anderson in *The Horn Book* points to Uncle Zeka as "somewhat of a trickster, an embodiment of traditional folklore" (598). This is misleading. If there is any tricksterish scheming in the book, it is found within the author herself—the scheming that parcels out Western ignorance to the children who will lead the twenty-first century. But this idea is repeated in another review also, one that refers to Uncle Zeka as "a variation of the trickster hero who appears frequently in the folklore of southern Africa" (118). Is the critic actually thinking of Bra Spider-Anansi, the folk hero of Ghana, West Africa? This trickster has traveled across the seas and become part of the folk tradition of blacks in the diaspora but is not specifically associated with southern Africa.

Another confusing feature is embedded in the title: *Do You Know Me*. The familiar African quip—do you know me?—is used twice by Farmer; once when Uncle Zeka challenges the shopkeeper who has offended and embarrassed his niece by accusing her of smoking. (She has tried to purchase cigarettes for her uncle, as requested.) Having this example to follow, Tapiwa stares down her snobbish classmates with this retort in her mind. She is no longer cowed by arrogant peers who see her as a lower-class impostor in their elitist school. But one wonders what the author understands of the quip from an African viewpoint. People use it to make jokes, to taunt, to challenge, to confront, to pick a fight, and to hide their own fear (as in Tapiwa's case). But the title has little significance to the story as a whole. In fact the title is counterproductive because it stands as an unintentional irony: Farmer misinterprets African character, she does not "know" it—she does not pass along its varied and complex truths to the young reader.

Children may also misconstrue the meaning of the slapstick hospital scenes in which Zeka smuggles Tapiwa to her mother's ward. He comes across as a foolish carrier of folk medicine, since the author depicts the traditional African healer in unfavorable terms—he is a man whom Tapiwa is commanded to stay away from unless she is accompanied by an adult (75). Zeka also bestows on his sister-in-law a gift comprised of papayas, cakes, sausages, candies, grapes, sardines, and a cheese in a waxy red cover—all stolen from Aunt Rudo and Uncle Soso. Western children may not understand that sharing is an integral part of communal living and not something that Zeka would construe as unethical. The scene is played as pure farce, as an adventure of two naughty children who cannot grasp the seriousness of a life-threatening surgery. While they boost the morale of everyone in the ward, the reader knows that they may well be taking a risk with others' lives.

Farmer is praised by critics for "an astute ear for dialogue, a deft hand with plot twists and a keen, dry wit," but this unabashed approval really represents the totality of Western cynicism. The work only serves to widen the gap between Africa and the West, between trust and distrust. Book reviewers have been delighted with this first novel (commending it for its humor, seriousness, geniality, universality, marvelous characterization, cultural authenticity, etc.), but a similar pleasure can be seen in white audiences in relation to "blackface" minstrel shows. Writing about the "stage Negro," sociologist Alan Green asks: who would *not* feel affection for a "permanently visible and permanently inferior clown who posed no threat and desired nothing more than laughter and applause at his imbecile antics"? (395). Farmer has bestowed this kind of satisfaction on the neocolonialist book critic. She has had considerable help from illustrator Shelley Jackson.

Illustrations

Illustrator Shelley Jackson sometimes embellishes characterization and sometimes sticks faithfully to the image suggested by language. In portraying the nganga, the traditional healer, she extends Farmer's description with harsh exaggerations, with perspective and tonal elements that make one think of the grotesque German expressionist portraits of the post–World War I era. Her treatments of Tapiwa and Uncle Zeka are cartoonish and follow closely the word-portraits created by the author. Aunt Rudo is given special attention, is characterized in the same hatefully stereotypic terms as nineteenth- and twentieth-century black women. Farmer sets the stage here by stressing Aunt Rudo's bulk (she cannot sit down without having "two chairs" placed in front of her). Also her gluttony is emphasized, as when she enjoys a picnic lunch consisting of "sausage rolls, potato salad, fried chicken, potato chips, cold ham, ... candied sweet potatoes ... cream puffs, apple pie, and chocolate brownies" (22). To see sketches of blacks with similar obese and negative features, one need only turn to children's books published from the mid-nineteenth to the mid-twentieth centries.* Farmer piles on the disgusting features of Aunt Rudo (e.g., her crocodile purse "is loaded with perfumes, makeup, and chocolate bars"), and Jackson represents all this with body language that denotes a domineering, conceited, cruel-hearted personality.

The *Publishers Weekly* critic saw another set of images—pictures that are described as "spirited black-and-white illustrations [that] exhibit a distinctive personality of their own while adding zest to this pair's adventures" (89). To be charmed by a minstrel-like figure—a "permanently inferior clown"—is to be charmed by its pictorial representative.

Conclusion

We close with a look at Farmer's finale. She transports Zeka to a distant laboratory where a Dr. Chirundu will be his caretaker. The doctor appears appreciative of the talents of his new assistant; he calls Zeka "a national treasure," a man who "knows the *uses* of everything he sees" (100). But the reader has *seen* on practically every page the uses that Uncle Zeka makes of things. The texture of the whole novel proclaims that this bush-village-bumpkin needs constant surveillance. Is the doctor really a "shrink" who tries to put a good face on the situation for the sake of the child? Tapiwa will never again be allowed to see this dear relative. "Tapiwa knew that her father's car was too old to make such a difficult trip again" (100). From an African perspective such a plot development is unthinkable. Africans who have not sold their birthright to colonialist impostors do not need a car to visit their relatives even if they are living in the very back of the beyond. Africans do not forget where their roots and umbilical cord are buried.

The saying "Do you know me?" could be construed as a sad and ironic inquiry since the Euro-American has never become acquainted with the African. Admittedly, however, some Africans have become puppets of neocolonialists, have acquired multiple complexes and the need

*See Simple Addition by a Little Nigger. *Uncle John's Drolleries. New York: McLoughlin Bros. [18—]; Edward Kemble's* Comical Coons. *New York: R.H. Russell, Publisher, 1898; Edward Kemble's drawings for the Autograph Edition of* Adventures of Huckleberry Finn, *New York: Harper, 1889; and Blanche Seale Hunt's* Stories of Little Brown Koko *(illustrated by Dorothy Wagstaff). Chicago & New York: American Colortype Co., 1953.*

to "find out who they are." Perhaps the best defense against this crisis in identity is to revisit the wisdom of the folk:

—Choose your love, and then love your choice.

—Mistakes are not haystacks or there would be more fat ponies.

—The strength of the hoe is tested on the soil.

—African and African-American proverbs

Works Cited

Anderson, Lois F. Rev. of *Do You Know Me* by Nancy Farmer. *Horn Book* 69:5 (Oct. 1993): 597.

Del Negro, Janice. Rev. of *Do You Know Me* by Nancy Farmer. *Booklist* 89:15 (April 1, 1993): 1431.

Duncan, Hugh Dalziel. *Communication and Social Order*. New York: Bedminster Press, 1962.

Farmer, Nancy. *Do You Know Me*. Illustrated by Shelley Jackson. New York: Orchard Books, 1993.

Green, Alan W. C. "'Jim Crow,' 'Zip Coon': The Northern Origins of Negro Minstrelsy." *Massachusetts Review* 11 (Spring, 1970): 385–97.

Miller-Lachmann, Lyn. Rev. of *Do You Know Me* by Nancy Farmer. *School Library Journal* 39:4 (April, 1993): 118.

Publishers Weekly. Rev. of *Do You Know Me* by Nancy Farmer. 240 (March 15, 1993): 88–9.

Tools of Distortion

Award-Winning Books about Blacks from South Africa and Great Britain*

Children's books that distort history and malign non–Western cultures receive inordinate praise in the current children's book world. They receive awards designating them "the best." This misplaced preeminence calls for a response from both cultural historians and children's literature specialists. It represents a trend that has not changed despite the new receptivity to black writers in the 1960s and beyond. The highest forms of prestige have been generally attached to works that misrepresent history, character, and culture, as seen in two artistic prizes awarded in the 1990s: the South African Sanlam Prize for Youth Literature for Michael Williams' *Into the Valley* (1993) and the British Whitbread prize for Peter Dickinson's *AK* (1992).

Both authors seem to share a common esprit de corps in dealing with the so-called black race "problem." Each book portrays Africans as largely chaotic, disorganized, irresponsible, and devoid of common sense and common humanity. Based on these assumed maladies, plots, characterizations, and stylistic features perpetuate a neocolonialist mindset that pits one group against another and implies white superiority.

On the book cover of *AK*, we read the blemished thoughts of an African boy warrior as conceived in the novel by his creator, Peter Dickinson: "'My mother was the war,' he [Paul] thought. 'She was a witch, a terrible demon, eater of people, but she looked after me. It's not my fault that I loved her.'" This quote illustrates the mental image that Dickinson wants to keep alive in an assumed Caucasian readership. The plot revolves around the self-destroying conflict referred to here as "the war."

*Parts of this essay were originally published in The Journal of African Children's and Youth Literature (JACYL), vol.6 (1994/95), and it is reprinted here with permission from JACYL. This presentation is in slightly expanded form.

As if by connivance, the inside cover of *Into the Valley* alerts the reader to anticipate a similar self-annihilating African community and the intervention of a "Tarzan" savior: "Heroes come in the unlikeliest forms and appear at the strangest times." Author Michael Williams substitutes the jungle hero with a white South African adolescent who sees himself mediating the rivalry between the African National Congress and the Inkatha Freedom Party. Both *Into the Valley* and *AK* reveal the many masks of neocolonialism.

Into the Valley: *Freedom Fighters as Youthful Warlords*

A traditional imperialist message pervades *Into the Valley*—namely, that Africans cannot do anything without outside help. Author Michael Williams interweaves his rite-of-passage scenario with events in Natal in the 1980s, especially the ANC/Inkatha dispute. His white South African hero, Walter Hudson, is a sixteen-year-old who journeys into the Shongweni Valley in search of his identity and some means for understanding his brother's death. (The latter has blown himself up in the midst of a prank played on fellow soldiers.) Walter has seen a news clipping describing ANC fighters of his own age, and he is especially inspired by reports of the leader named Biko, a youngster named in honor of the real Steve Biko (an anti–Apartheid activist slain by South African police).

The real Biko did not set himself up to be a hero or martyr, but Williams apparently felt the need to create a Western media Biko-type: a boy guerrilla leading other boys. In his bid to discredit the Steve Biko image, Williams portrays the gang as one that takes bribes from a Western investor. Using the white teenager's point of view, the author introduces readers to a cross-section of indigenous and colonial townsfolk, but black African adults are conspicuous in their absence. They have fled in the face of the adolescent vigilantes, ANC members who terrorize others with demands for "protection" payments. This money is supposedly intended for use in chasing off Inkatha Party gangs. The political issue is described in terms of feuding clans and tribal violence, with no hint that a fight against apartheid is underway. Alice, a white girl used by the author to explain the fighting to Walter and to the reader, states: "'You start with one incident in a village ... and soon have a full-blown feud.... An eye for an eye. A tooth for a tooth'" (71). The "Biko"-led gang members unwittingly protect the interests of the Western colonials, while becoming destructive to their own parents, elders, and homeland. They are largely depicted as reckless thugs and bandits.

Williams suggests repeatedly that the black Africans have not a clue as to what is going on or why. The villagers have abandoned the region to the guerrilla "play" of the children and to a South African Defense Force commander who would solve the problem (so we are told) if people would just tell the truth and give him reliable information. James, a Westernized storekeeper who serves as another mouthpiece for the author, explains about the "faction fighting":

> "The African National Congress wants power and the Inkatha Freedom Party wants power. Members of the IFP come here and start talking to the villagers to try and get them to join. The ANC doesn't like it. But you ask one of the people—that woman, for example"—James pointed to the burned remains of the house with the blue door—"what the ANC stands for, and she hasn't a clue, not a clue!" [72].

This neocolonial perspective—that the black population is incompetent in dealing with civic and economic problems—is woven throughout the tale. For example, the Western investor who bribes the "Biko" gang is a sugar plantation owner who is importing laborers to defeat local unionization efforts, but the ANC is too naive to understand. The teenage guerrillas aid the anti-union forces, while only the visiting white teenager recognizes what is really happening. Through Walter's eyes the counterproductive action of the Africans becomes clear:

> He understood now that there were one or two charismatic, intelligent boys using their power to protect a village, and that they were, at the same time, using that power to exploit the people of the village. They, in turn, were being exploited by someone else [the sugar producers] [157].

This is turning history on its head. Union building and solidarity are not new or unfamiliar phenomena to South African blacks.

In the cultural sphere, a neocolonial viewpoint is presented in Williams' treatment of folklore. In a climactic scene, we see ANC youngsters flee in the face of an Inkatha assassination team (in the middle of a public street the team executes the town schoolmaster); ANC members hide in terror because someone has seen an owl fly over the teacher's house. "It is what my people believe," explains a gang member: that owls are a bad omen and any resistance is futile ("No one could save the teacher after *isikhova* had visited him" [150]). This reduces a traditional "bad luck" sign to an exercise in social irresponsibility. It makes African tradition a lethal carry-over from the past.

In numerous scenes the message relates to an implied "backwardness." An elderly woman is stubbornly determined to brew unhealthy beer. Young children with skin diseases are not treated except as part of a bribe to gain more supplies for the young guerrillas. A black mother needs Western indoctrination or she will abuse her baby with an unnourishing diet; additionally, she has no sense when it comes to handling money. James announces to the Western bystanders in his store:

> "Look at that woman. ... That baby is malnourished. I keep on trying to get her to buy food that will be good for it....." As he rang up the price [of a chicken] he said: "I told her to buy a whole chicken. It's cheaper and she can make soup from the leftovers. Look at this child. I'm sure it's not getting enough food, and there are many others like it" [73-74].

James, with his Western education, is portrayed as an all-purpose benefactor, but even he has a difficult time screwing up enough courage to face down the ANC extortioners. In this one character the author undermines the image of African manhood, while also suggesting that Western influences will redeem the African's weaknesses somewhat—the imperialist viewpoint in a nutshell.

While James epitomizes one aspect of colonized Africa, two black servants (Shadrach and Abednego) illustrate another form of propaganda. These characters are the means for mocking African character in a minstrel-like comedy act. McRory, a South African of Scottish descent, introduces his servants to Walter:

> Walter ... shook the limp hand offered self-consciously by the grinning man.
> "Shadrach, do you know what ANC means?" McRory asked.
> "No. Baas. Trouble, just trouble!" said Shadrach.
> "And Inkatha?"
> "More trouble. Big trouble."
> "Do you know what's going on up there?" McRory pointed to the distant hills.
> "Yes, Baas, fighting! Lots of fighting. Very bad people."
> McRory turned triumphantly to Walter.
> "You see what I mean? This guy's lived up there all his life and he has no idea what's going on" [54].

The ludicrous naming of the two servants illustrates the use of the "comic" stereotype to underscore so-called primitivism. The Bible reference is a typical minstrel-show device.

In contrast, young Walter is portrayed as a serious youth in search of purpose and stability. And although his search is simplistic, it becomes one strand in a story that implies much more. In short, the author takes the complex issues connected with the anti–Apartheid struggle and makes them a vehicle for colonialist attitudes. When you only take a piece of a person and disregard the rest, you are left with a simplified, one-dimensional image. That is what Williams does with the Africans in his novel.

AK: *The Futility of Positive Change*

Peter Dickinson's *AK* similarly allows for no range of human qualities in indigenous Africans—no ongoing political development, no grasp of historical causation. Tribalism is again treated as the unseen enemy, as a characteristic of a so-called primitive, underdeveloped consciousness. One character is presented as beyond this stage and working to achieve a sound post-colonial government, but he dies in the end. He is greatly outnumbered by the corrupt and even sadistic leaders of this mythical nation. Dickinson takes us from one coup d'etat to the next as he depicts the Africa of today as a place of doom and ignominy.

In a prefatory section, Dickinson explains the political-economic history of his imagined nation, "Nagala." He provides a mythical map and carefully documents the nation's origins by using situations that parallel the actual "scramble for Africa" among European nations in the late nineteenth century. While he alludes to British culpability in the evils of colonialism (e.g., the British used forced labor instead of slaves and "punitive expeditions" in place of "massacres"), his images of Africa are full of futility and scorn. Nagala, he writes, is "on no map of Africa, but it is there, this vast, poor country. For thousands of years it was no country, only tribes" (1). We learn that the first democratic government of Nagala "made a real mess of their job," even though the departing colonizers "explained to the people what a ballot box was, and a cabinet, and an opposition, and so on" (3,2). Given these put-downs, the reader will not find it too surprising that a military junta takes charge, then a guerrilla leader who permits rigged elections. Moreover, all the new political parties have "democratic-sounding names, all with different initials but all much the same, and between them almost as bad as Boyo [the military dictator], in different ways. The army did what it liked..." (3,4).

Dickinson adds various false impressions to this sardonic treatment of Africa. He claims that the British left because they worked out how much it was costing them, but if Nagala had really been such an enormous loss, the British would not have stayed for ten years let alone seventy. Additionally, the British, says Dickinson, found that democracy wasn't easy because there were many tribes, languages, and ways of life. He doesn't admit that if the Brits had established a democratic system of government, then languages and lifestyles would not have presented problems that were insurmountable. Dickinson admits in a footnote that people with different home languages got along in "naga," while townspeople often spoke English (3). Communication was not the problem, nor was it true that every educated African was a doctor or lawyer and had not learned "how to run an agricultural improvements scheme, or a road maintenance department" (3). Dickinson's colonizer perspective will simply not allow a capacity for good judgment within the African population, nor will the author admit that African resistance movements had anything to do with national liberation. Actually most colonial powers did not find it too easy to bring the colonized into subjugation, nor did they enjoy ongoing acquiescence on the part of Africans. When most of the imperial powers had to leave, it was a struggle; some left in a hurry, some in humiliation, some in disgrace. Only a few departed as friends.

In portraying his leading players—Paul (a guerrilla fighter even at the tender age of eight years) and Jilli (an adolescent girl from a rural village)—Dickinson resorts to stock characters. Jilli has a genius for imitation, but although she can mimic a BBC announcer, she is quite indifferent about learning the meaning of English words or words spoken by friends from other African groups. She typically behaves like an infant, doting on Western symbols such as blue jeans, high heels, and sports cars, even though she is on the verge of womanhood. Her role seems to be in supplying "comic" relief; she is the funny "native" whose childishness is not much different from the immaturity assigned to blacks in nineteenth century imperialist novels. This degrading treatment of a young woman is hard to synchronize with Dickinson's description of himself and his work as a novelist: "I regard myself as a feminine chap.... I write in the women's voices" (Lipsom, 30).

Paul is central to the story as the child victim—a youngster who knows only the war as his "mother" and whose obsessive attachment to his AK rifle constitutes the book's continuing metaphor. Paul and Jilli have the resilience of the young, and in one of two endings that Dickinson writes into this parable, Paul lives happily as a game warden while Jilli wins acclaim as a film director. In ending "B" Paul dies at the hands of new child-warriors. Some reviewers have seen these two opposite endings as instructive, as "showing the concerns facing many Third World countires" and offering readers a chance to consider "how we in the 'First World' should react" (Forman, 90). Apparently this critic is oblivious to those people outside the "First World" and their participation as readers.

If these opposite endings presented a real choice, the parable might be instructive to the young, but Dickinson "stacks the deck" with his overwhelmingly negative images of Africa. He depicts an ancient land whose people are incapable of adapting in the way societies typically adapt to change. The people know how to create underwater fences to protect their buffalo from crocodiles and they use mud as a mosquito repellent, but nothing has prepared them for urban development and economic diversification. Africa, it seems, was not ready for the departure of its Western overseers!

Group portraits reinforce this image of arrested development whether the portrait delineates the masses, the government forces, or the rebels. The shantytowns had the "smell of hopelessness in the air almost as strong as the smells of rot and dirt.... All those people! They should have been a great power, ... but they lay here rotting and listless, hundreds of thousands of meaningless lives, like the marshes below Tsheba" (150). Sadistic acts are common within the military, as when a truck of soldiers is seen with the body of a man lashed to its fender. "The dangling arm bore a corporal's stripes. The lolling head was bare, its black curls soaked with blood. Paul had seen bodies like that before [when] ... soldiers had come through [a village] picking out men at random and 'executing' them" (132). As for the rebels, they would "rape [women and girls] as soon as look at them," and young boys (like Paul) were not any safer (26).

This assumption of unreadiness for membership in the modern world denies Africa its historical evolution and dynamic social consciouness, and yet this interpretation is not uncommon in the Western media. In Western news reports, European withdrawal from the African continent has been implicitly treated as untimely if not misguided. After the conflict in Zaire in 1978, an Associated Press reporter made this sweeping appraisal: "[The continent] suffers from the effects of the vacuum left when the European colonial powers withdrew.... The key element in all this remains tribalism" (Kaba, 43). Regional cooperation is not treated as a possibility because so-called primitivism precludes historical change. On the other hand, longstanding European conflicts, whether among the

Irish, Basques, or Serbs, are not subjected to such biased generalizations. Nor is the violent bomb culture of Europe and America treated with the same level of censure as killings and deprivations experienced by Aficans.

Both alternative endings in the novel have a neocolonialist tinge. The choice between ending "A" and ending "B" is largely a choice between Africans-as-entertainers and Africans-as-terrorists. The "happy" ending is presented first; Paul has become a game-park warden, Jilli is a globe-trotting film director, and their friend Francis is the deputy prime minister of the nation. In celebrating the installation of a monument, Paul and Francis amble through the park:

> The sigh of happiness came as the path turned and the view opened below them, mile after mile of brown bush mottled with flat-topped trees, hazy with heat, yearning for the rains…. Half a mile away five elephants loitered beneath a stand of tamarisks [223].

By the time Europeans firmly established their rule over Africa, imperialism became transformed into "natural history" (Pieterse, 95–96). Game parks as well as museums became trophies of European victory. They were a satisfying symbol of the pacification of Africa, the end of viable resistance on the part of the Africans. Paul is situated in a non-threatening role in this "happy" scenario (a role that was "his dream," as it was "the dream" of his surrogate parent, Michael Kagomi, according to Dickinson).

Paul is devoted to his job as keeper of the Europeans' playground, while Jilli is the impulsive child even in adult life. She occupies another nonthreatening position vis-à-vis the colonial vision for Africa. Paul reports to Francis: "She called last week from Bangkok. She's fallen in love again—didn't say who with" (222). Is Jilli a perennial adolescent or the stereotypically promiscuous black woman? And why does Dickinson depict even the deputy prime minister as a man with a "babylike face" (221)?

Ending "A" puts all the Africans in their "place," while it also tells of the burial of the AK-47 rifle beneath twelve tons of concrete. Peace is now being waged but the terms do not suggest African strength, maturity, or self-realization.

In ending "B" Paul Kagomi is killed by a member of the succeeding generation of preadolescent "freedom fighters." Nagala is the site of endless wars. Michael [Kagomi] has been "gunned down outside his cheap hotel in London"; Madam Ga has been "strangled in her own house by 'burglars'"; Francis Papp has "disappeared into a government camp"; and

Jilli "simply disappeared" (227). Paul is on the same side of the conflict as the people who kill him, but he is negligent in that he is walking in a certain region and "shouldn't have been here without clearing it through HQ" (229). As in all parts of this novel, Africans with power are depicted as despots and incapable of responsible action.

"Africa's recovery," writes historian Basil Davidson, "will have to be, essentially, the fruit of Africa's own history" (278). Postcolonial independence implies that Africans will have to be treated as people, and from this premise it follows that African history must be understood. Davidson asks, "Where ... had they come from? What had they done, or not done, before the colonial invasions of the 1850s and later? What, in a word, had been their history?" (99). The self-serving answer of the colonizer had been that Africa had no history before the coming of the whites, that "Africa had stayed ... in featureless stagnation, lost to every stirring of the human mind" (Davidson, 100). It is this sense of stagnation that Dickinson reinforces with his alternate visions: Africa as "park" or Africa as "battlefield."

A real alternate vision would include an African-based political renewal. It would concede the point made by Nigerian economist and reformer Adebayo Adedeji: "There can be no doubt that Africa needs a new political order which breaks the umbilical cord from its unenviable colonial inheritance" (Quoted in Davidson, 251). The forces that comprise that colonial inheritance are never allowed to surface in this novel: the problem of growth without accompanying economic development and the problem of independence without national security. Africa's uneven relationship with the outside world's economy and political clout are not offered as background information. The failure to supply this necessary context hardly bothers the Western public consciousness, but Dickinson has described himself as a person "concerned about social justice and the maiming of the future" (Commire, 56). Is a message implying African stagnation and dependency the best we can expect from a Western, self-professed liberal?

Davidson is one of Dickinson's British compatriots, but he brings a different legacy into the foreground: "...there remains, in the ethos of African community, a fountain of inspiration, a source of civility, a power of self-correction, and ... these are qualities that may yet be capable ... of vital acts of restitution" (290). Additionally, the point is made that "pre-colonial statecraft built successful independent states," and although we are in a vastly changed world, this precedent serves as an important "paradigm of popular participation" in government (*Modern Africa*, 276). Unfortunately, the professional book-reviewing press too often shares Dickinson's neocolonialist vision.

Reviews and Reviewers

Before the awarding of prizes, there is often a gradual accumulation of favorable opinion expressed for a particular title through the popular and professional press. A review is, therefore, not important merely for its appraisal but for the growing momentum that is building on behalf of a given work. In other words, canon-development is a joint enterprise shared by professional critics and the juries responsible for bestowing literary awards. The market for a book increases as its "blue ribbon" status becomes known.

Reviews of the works under discussion here were generally supportive and point to a unified perspective among authors, publishers, and critics. Reviewers usually sided with authors in seeing Africa as its own worst enemy. They seemed to concur in the impression that indigenous African cultures and institutions are obstacles to progressive change, that they leave Africa ill-prepared for good government, civic order, and social harmony.

Reviews of *AK* are a case in point. They credit Dickinson with total journalistic reliability. Critic Michele Slung, writing in the *New York Times Book Review*, says that the author's mythical kingdom of Nagala "is no more outlandish than one we might encounter by boarding an airplane" (33). She notes that Dickinson transforms "the familiar," as if his contrivances were as observable as those that could be actually documented. The plot, according to the reviewer, centers upon a transition from wartime to peacetime. In particular, the storyline focuses upon this issue: "How will a twelve-year-old adapt to peace when his childhood existence has depended upon survival skills within a guerrilla war setting?"

This question is never really unanswered for long because political factions in Dickinson's Africa are portrayed as incapable of waging peace. "Tribal hostilities," says Slung, and their accompanying "political intrigues" are "as dangerous as ever." Dickinson is praised for his "splendidly moving spectacle" of a mass uprising, a rebellion that ushers in the next cyclical interlude of nation-building. But then Dickinson is applauded for showing that this newfound hope is "never certain" because, apparently, Nagala's character does not permit stability. In an African setting, overthrowing a government of "thugs" is an operation too fragile to sustain hope. Slung concludes: "the ultimate fate of Nagala ... or of places like it, can never be certain, and Mr. Dickinson carefully structures his conclusion so the lesson of ambiguity is the one we carry away" (33).

Having a basic agreement about so-called "tribalism" and "intrigue," both critic and author prescribe the expected outcome: "a lesson of ambiguity." To predict stability in Africa would be an exercise in wishful thinking according to the neocolonialist worldview.

The Horn Book Magazine repeats the idea that what Dickinson writes is to be accepted as historical reality. Critic Margaret A. Bush states at the outset that "the events are so true to those in several parts of the contemporary world that this novel becomes a parable for our time" (588). The story "is disturbing in its plausibility"; it explores the "dynamics of war." The problem with this assessment is that "plausibility" is not a term that could by any means be applied unless one were first to assume that Dickinson's one-sided portrait of Africa is credible. The novelist treats cruelty and a disregard for human life as the norm in African society; he describes opponents to this way of life as too few to serve as a basis for African self-determination. As a whole the novel is a thinly disguised justification for colonialism, and American critics are buying into that theme without questioning it.

In *Booklist*, reviewer Hazel Rochman describes the plot of *AK* as "like a documentary." She objects to two-dimensionality in the depiction of character but ends her review with the judgment that "the best parts of the book are the introductory chapter with its bitter history of Africa and then the two alternative endings" (1520). "Bitterness" may be an apt term for what Dickinson puts on display, but to talk about the history of Africa without pinpointing actual components of that history is to leave readers with a "blame-the-victim" message. The self-destructiveness of Dickinson's Africa distracts from the actual historical causes underlying African dislocations, in particular the dislocations resulting from Western imperialism.

Michael Williams' *Into the Valley* received ecstatic praise in the South African press but a mixed response in American children's book journals. Quoted on the book's cover is the endorsement of the *Book Chat Review* of Cape Town: "Brilliant ... it mesmerises." The *Cape Times* noted that "*Into the Valley* is a very promising and gripping novel." The *Natal Witness* called it a "must": "Williams writes with a fluent skill.... A must for any young reader." Such unabashed enthusiasm was repeated in the University of Illinois' *Bulletin of the Center for Children's Books*. Professor Selma K. Richardson noted with approval a "splendid sense of confusion" in Williams' treatment of ANC-Inkatha violence. Life in the Illongweni Valley, according to Richardson, was delineated as "clear and true" (26, 27).

Less laudatory critics mention the implausibilities in the plot and the author's unsuccessful experiment with a shifting narrative voice. Neocolonialist elements are largely passed over. The *Publishers Weekly* reviewer calls the novel a "morality play about factional fighting among blacks" but is primarily upset about "stock characters" and a "clumsy" narrative technique (71-72). Only Hazel Rochman appropriately takes Williams to task for writing "as if Apartheid has just vanished." In her *Booklist* critique, she also notes how improbable is the portrait of a white protagonist who enters the valley without "a vestige of prejudice" (2051). What needs a more thorough probing is the stereotyping of blacks and the countless improvisations on the theme of white superiority.

Conclusion

Literary misrepresentations of Africans warrant close examination and active opposition. Yet prize-winners such as those critiqued here are widely circulating throughout the world, while, ironically, Africanists are examining in their conferences such topics as "Post-Apartheid Literature" and "Pan Africanism Updated." If an "update" is to be meaningful—if strategies for change are to be effective—serious consideration needs to be given to the way young white minds are being nurtured to think that "white" is superior and invincible. Similarly, Africanist scholars should feel obliged to confront the manner in which young black minds are being instilled with the myth that an endemic "primitivism" characterizes people of African descent.

Writing about literary untruths in the adult book world, Chinweizu, Jemie, and Madubuike refer to the need for an "intellectual and cultural bush clearing." They do not relish the task. They express the wish that "such bush clearing work were unnecessary." However, they add that "given the havoc wrought by imperialist hegemony over our [African] culture, it [is] unavoidable" (304). The "havoc" represented by the miseducation of children is of even greater import given the obstinacy of impressions formulated in childhood. Currently, children are reared to act out continuing intergroup conflict rather than enjoy the richness and security of a world in which difference does not imply superiority or inferiority or "even any ranking at all" (Chinweizu, 302). The mutuality and camaraderie of *this* world is the child's true birthright.

Works Cited

Bush, Margaret A. Rev. of *AK* by Peter Dickinson. *Horn Book* 65 (Sept/Oct, 1992): 588.

Chinweizu, Onwuchekwa Jemie, and Ihechukwu Madubuike. *The Decolonization of African Literature.* Enugu, Nigeria: Fourth Dimension Publishers, 1980.

Commire, Anne, ed. "Peter Dickinson." *Something About the Author.* V. 5. Detroit: Gale Research, 1973.

Davidson, Basil. *Modern Africa.* 3d ed. London and New York: Longman, 1994.

_____. *The Search for Africa: A History in the Making.* London: James Currey, 1994.

Dickinson, Peter. *AK.* New York: Delacorte Press, 1992,

Forman, Jack. Rev. of *AK* by Peter Dickinson. *School Library Journal* 38 (July, 1992): 90.

Kaba, Lansine. "Historical Consciousness and Politics in Africa." In *Black Studies: Theory, Method, and Cultural Perspectives.* Ed. Talmadge Anderson. Pullman: Washington State University Press, 1990: pp. 43-51

Lipsom, Eden Ross. "Write, Research, Then Rewrite." *New York Times Book Review* April 20, 1986; p. 30.

Pieterse, Jan Nederveen. *White on Black: Images of Africa and Blacks in Western Popular Culture.* New Haven: Yale University Press, 1992.

Review of *Into the Valley* by Michael Williams. *Publishers Weekly* 240:24 (June 14, 1993): 71–72.

Richardson, Selma K. Rev. of *Into the Valley* by Michael Williams. *The Bulletin of the Center for Children's Books* 47:1 (September, 1993): 26–27.

Rochman, Hazel. Rev. of *AK* by Peter Dickinson. *Booklist* (April 15, 1992): 1520.

_____. Rev. of *Into the Valley* by Michael Williams. *Booklist* 89 (August, 1993): 2051.

Slung, Michele. Rev. of *AK* by Peter Dickinson. *New York Times Book Review.* Sept. 27, 1992; p. 33.

Williams, Michael. *Into the Valley.* New York: Philomel Books, 1993.

Teenage Trauma and South African "Street People"

Coming-of-Age Novels in an African Context

"If art may dispense with the constraining exactitude of literal truth," writes Chinua Achebe, "it does acquire in return incalculable powers of persuasion in the imagination" (138). "[A novel] though invented, has the power to ring true," writes Elizabeth Bowen. And she adds, "It does not merely invent ... it intensifies, therefore it gives power, extra importance, greater truth ... to what well may be ordinary" (114). "The truths" of modern times include such disparate phenomena as teenage trauma, the racism of Apartheid, and the struggle to dismantle it. Yet in the young adult novel they often merge. Authors place family members in conflict with one another over Apartheid; they profile the police abuses in the townships; they feature young gangs or young political activists. Being faithful to teenage psychology is one artistic necessity in such novels, and being faithful to sociopolitical conditions is another.

In *Crocodile Burning* (1992), author Michael Williams produces a confused and biased picture of South Africa. He employs a first-person black voice and then contradicts what his teenage narrator stands for by masking an essentially pro–Apartheid argument with anti–Apartheid generalizations. This sleight-of-hand creates a classic case of disjuncture between form and content. Soweto's anti–Apartheid struggles are central to the content, while the form of the novel (its characterizations and descriptive texture) takes a blame-the-victim approach. While the author is telling us that Apartheid is bad, he is also strongly implying that black rule would be worse. He revolves his plot around two black characters: Seraki, a young, alienated petty criminal, and Mosake, a playwright and theater director who recruits Seraki for a musical show and takes the play to Broadway. Ultimately, Mosake cheats, manipulates, intimidates, and assaults the young members of his cast in utter contradiction to his play, which is an anti–Apartheid narrative.

83

Isezela (the crocodile) refers to a character in many traditional African myths. Williams describes it as a monster with the power to startle and confuse: "This old, evil crocodile lies in shallow water ready to attack the innocent." In the creative mind of Mosake, the *isezela* becomes a powerful image intended to carry the message of his musical drama. The traditional and modern are juxtaposed; both are conceptualized as having the same shape. We imagine, therefore, that the old monster crocodile and a plastic model are intrinsically connected. Mosake tells his young cast members:

> This is a plastic toy [crocodile]. … Our country is filled with plastic crocodiles: the old traditions that enslave our people, the education system, the government and its policies, detention without trial, the state of emergency, and the crime and violence in our townships [32–33].

The plastic *isezela* is an appropriate symbol because of what it should represent—namely, advanced technology, gang crimes, and exploitative values that thrive on shrewd, scheming, acquisitive desires. It represents the ever-increasing capitalist profiteering that has become Africa's cancer. The reader is probably aware of *this* monster and its power to lie in wait within geographical borders. But could *isezela* also be an effective symbol for that which must defend itself? The young people of South Africa have initiated boycotts, strikes, and other open confrontations with the dreaded Apartheid system; but are they now being set up to be exploited like their parents and parents' parents? And is this to be at the hands of a black man—a playwright with the tongue of an iguana and the character of a chameleon? Mosake, as an African and an artist, knows what it means to speak a true word, to state a worthy ideal. He gives his young actors this important message in his play: "'We're taught what you want to teach us. We learn what you want us to learn. But we cannot live as you want us to live!'" (38). But Mosake's role in the novel embodies the attitude, personality, and lifestyle of the neocolonialist African missionary salesman. His role is typical of the successful "middleman," whose faceless partners in business, exploitation, and extortion in Africa are protected by both domestic and foreign interests.

Williams makes the character of Mosake central in this story, eclipsing Apartheid and the anti–Apartheid struggle. He asks the reader to take a good critical look and evaluate black-on-black interactions, instead of always accusing the whites and their racist policies. "Art," wrote Struthers Burt, "is selection, concentration, and direction on the part of [a writer]" (196). The way Williams sets the direction of the narrative is by lining up violent acts by blacks. The government security forces lock people away when they are student resisters, but the actual blood spilled in the book is the result of black-on-black violence. Moreover, the black youth gangs are depicted as *anti–Apartheid* activists, who nonetheless murder, burn, extort, and rape the Sowetan townsfolk. This is where the author places his concentration, and passing references to Nelson Mandela or to Seraki's heroic brother (who is in jail without being charged) do not counter-balance the sadism of the street people or the domestic quarrels and hatred in Seraki's family. A few liberal code words do not offset the cruelties that constitute the texture of the work.

Conspicuous Black-on-Black Cruelties

"Design, in fiction," writes Zona Gale, "is theme treated with heightened awareness" (35). The weight Williams attaches to black-on-black violence lends credibility to stereotypes and to *pro*–Apartheid arguments (to fears of anarchy, vengeance, ungovernability, and so on). Abstractly the author salutes Mandela, but he gives his readers no opportunity to identify with him. "Fiction ... is the fruit of perfect self-identification of the writer with his [her] materials — with beings, with situations, with objects, with time and place" (Gale, 35). Williams builds a framework of negative identification.

In the first half of the novel, the "Naughty Boys" are the principal antagonists, alongside Seraki's father, "Mr. Nzule." In 1986, "the year of the troubles," various work stoppages were organized, resulting in the government's declaration of a State of Emergency. Describing this history, Williams relates how street gangs (the "Boys") enforced the boycott by injuring Seraki's mother:

> They said she mustn't go to her job. Going to work was against their orders. They said people who went to work were supporting the system of Apartheid. They forced her to eat the soap powder she had bought from a white man's shop. She was sick for a long time after that [21].

As part of this violent enforcement of "solidarity" on behalf of democracy, the "Naughty Boys" extort money. When Seraki's uncle believes he has located Phakane (Seraki's brother) and takes Seraki to visit him in prison (a futile journey as it turns out), the "Boys" are not pleased:

> "You come asking for information, we give it to you on condition you pay us, and then you try to sneak away.... You want to see your nephew,

you pay us the money." He slams the ax into the table. With his big hands moving fast, he pulls at my uncle's hair, forces him down onto the table, pries loose the ax, and passes it to one of the other men.... He is holding Uncle's neck, squashing his face into the table. Then he ... nods to the man with the ax. It crashes down in front of my uncle's face [51–52].

When Seraki's father arrives, they twist his arm and "push his face next to Uncle's." The leader "pulls Uncle's face off the table and slams it back down" (52). By the end of the scene, blood is smeared all over both men, Uncle is blamed for everything, and Seraki's father drives him from the house at knife point. When a neighbor disobeys the "pro-democracy" vigilantes, a petrol bomb is thrown into his house and he is assassinated when he makes his exit. This, we are told, is common practice. No forces in the community are working to stem this violence; adults are paralyzed in the face of adolescent bullies. They take no action when young school-girls are taken from their classrooms by the "Boys" and raped. This, we are told, is common practice. "This happens in the township a lot.... The gangs come looking for schoolgirls and nobody stops them. Not the principals, not the police, not anybody. Nobody dares" (58). Black violence is coupled with black passivity; on both counts the indigenes come across as incapable of self-determination, self-rule, or even self-preservation.

"Mr. Nzuke," Seraki's father, is the second antagonist in the early part of the book and embodies a second set of stereotypes. Seraki uses the "Mister" as a sign of ironic disrespect. Although Seraki has an affectionate attachment to his maternal uncle, this fact does not counteract culturally his strange attitude towards his father. The son is aware of "Mr. Nzuke's" many problems: his joblessness, his confrontations with the police, his incarceration—the way he has been stripped of his manhood, respect, honor, and dignity. That Mr. Nzuke demanded respect when he came out of prison seems like a too-fragile excuse for the rift between father and son. The fact that he is accused of womanizing, drinking too much, and abusively taking his frustrations out on his wife all suggest a ploy to discredit the male as irresponsible.

Additionally, the author characterizes Mr. Nzule with an irrational resentment toward his wife's brother. This belies one of the most fundamental beliefs of the African—namely, the importance of warm and hospitable interactions. On this point, anti–Apartheid martyr Steve Biko has written: "One of the most fundamental aspects of our culture is the importance we attach to Man." (Biko uses the term generically.) "Intimacy is a term not exclusive for particular friends but applying to a whole group of people who find themselves together. ... No one felt unnecessarily an intruder into someone else's business. The curiosity manifested was welcome. It came out of a desire to share" (41-42). It is therefore surprising that in the novel Mr. Nzule would drive his wife's brother from the house, knowing he had come a long way to visit not only his sister but friends and the entire family.

It is this cultural unity, this communal bonding that Mosake will exploit. He knows he can obtain such a bond from the youngsters in his play. He also knows that he can sell it to the capitalist market as art. He can use African music and dance as a commodity, while he is himself alienated from his roots. In African culture, music and dance are not luxuries but an integral part of communication. Love, death, suffering, working—these are all made real through song, dance, and rhythm. Seraki's uncle plays the saxophone and makes people laugh and feel happy. Mosake does not laugh easily. He achieves success with his play but gets rid of the very people who have once helped him. He has acquired the tricks and schemes of the plastic *isezela*. He is aggressive and devious.

Williams contrives in Mosake a character who is worse than the many plastic crocodiles that have come to invade South Africa. Like the invading settlers he travels with a *sjambok* (a whip). He uses it as the colonizer-settler used it: mercilessly. When Seraki and a fellow actor are mugged and forced to make the show open late, Mosake unleashes his wrath on them. The playwright/impressario's response is totally irrational, but designed to frighten the youngsters into a slavish submission to his will:

> We are under the stage, below the boiler room, under the earth, in his lair. There are no windows, only blackness, the wandering beam of light, this smell ["the rotting, dark, moldering smell of death"], and him.... He's dragged us down to a black hole under the theater. He's hidden us, thrown us away. He's leaving us to rot.... He stands over me with his *sjambok* raised.... I wince away from the *sjambok*. He waits for me to relax, then he will lash out [140-41].

Ultimately, Seraki and his friends burn the toy crocodile in a rooftop ceremony in Manhattan, and some of their "Subsistence and Travel" money that Mosake has stolen is recovered. But everyone agrees to keep the scandal secret and Mosake's reputation as South Africa's great black theatrical genius is not to be tarnished. The novel ends with this white-collar criminal alive and well—still planning to open in an extended run of the play and with whatever cast members wish to sign on again. Whether Seraki will join again is left ambiguous.

As for the leader of the "Naughty Boys," he is given a five-year jail sentence for peddling drugs. His cohorts, apparently, are still on the loose on Soweto street corners. Only Mandela's release from prison offers a sign of hope.

Williams attempts to repudiate Apartheid, but he builds a scenario that in effect supports it. "The artist," writes Struthers Burt, "has to have his urge toward self-expression definitely channeled, directed, and in constant motion toward an end; ... The force of what he says ... is the result of the compression of channeling, or discipline" (195). The path of Williams' novel, the channel, is at odds with its outcome. The pattern is full of contradictions. Nor has he set out to educate Western teenagers. His characters carry the message-image that will sell to a select Western audience.* It is impossible to dialogue when exploitative methods become instruments of education.

Trauma in Suburbia: Rosenthal's Wake Up Singing

Fiction about South Africa, mostly the work of Caucasian writers, has been plentiful in recent years. The near-explosive political situation promised clashes that could be woven into a drama of fever-pitched suspense. Jane Rosenthal's *Wake Up Singing* (1990) seems to try to project a

---

*Western critics were "sold," as seen in the following remarks by reviewers: "a worthwhile and compelling read," "the township and its people are powerfully portrayed," "the motif of the crocodile is skillfully woven into the plot," "good pacing and the first-person, present-tense narrative give the events immediacy." (See School Library Journal, 38:11, Nov., 1992.) The Kirkus review (60:13, July 1, 1992) notes that "the author's theatrical experience stands him in good stead" and that "Williams' insider's view of South Africa will open some eyes." The Horn Book reviewer said the novel was "as current and vivid as today's news headlines" (68:5, Sept./Oct. 1992). "An important addition to school and public library collections" said the VOYA critic (15:4, Oct. 1992). "A worthwhile and compelling read," according to Susan Giffard in School Library Journal (38:11, Nov., 1992). An "important contribution to literature written for all adolescents," said the reviewers for Journal of Reading (36:7, April 1993). And the American Library Association selected the novel as a "Best Book for Young Adults." All these accolades bring to mind Chinua Achebe's observation that "white racism against Africa is such a normal way of thinking that its manifestations go completely unremarked." (See Hopes and Impediments; Selected Essays. New York: Doubleday, 1989; p. 12.)

"thinking voice," a "new revolutionary" attitude toward Apartheid.* This new thinking is embodied in Nick Mackenzie, a senior white pupil in an all-white school; his parents are colonial white settlers living in the white suburbs far removed from the black townships. Rosenthal's gentlemanly domestic arguments and quarrels would not have existed had there been no Apartheid, no superficial political situation impinging on the protected homes and schools of the whites. Nick's various traumas—his quarrel with his father about assisting black fugitives, his dismissal from the cadet corps and the shame of being forced to strip down in front of his classmates, his two-week stint of volunteer work at a township church—do not seem to properly fit in a jigsaw puzzle that involves the very safety of human lives.

The black child did not wake up singing; he/she did not know a secure life. Blacks did not know if they would survive the day or end up in jail. As Steve Biko told the court in his own trial: black South Africans are "oppressed by an external world through institutionalised machinery, through laws that restrict [them] from doing certain things, through heavy work conditions, … through poor education" (100). The black child/youth had no alternative but to protest, to defy and confront the forces of subjugation. By reversing anti–Apartheid roles and responsibilities, Rosenthal is playing a dangerous game of hijacking. Roles of responsibility in the Apartheid situation cannot be made into a casual game of hide-and-seek love play—the basic plot device for connecting Nick with the pro-democracy struggle.

The storyline places Nick, Em (the love interest), and Em's brother Theo on the white side, and they are brought together with Zach and Mapho on the black side. But the way Zach and Mapho are presented in the novel does not put in perspective for the reader anything about what the blacks have in common with Nick and his friends. Why should they trust each other given the tense situation? It would seem that if Zach and Mapho are to be recognized as "good," they must associate with the Nicks, Ems, and Theos. Biko addressed this psychological form of oppression: "the black man [sic] in himself has developed a certain state of alienation, he rejects himself, precisely because he attaches the meaning white to all that is good…. This … arises out of his development from childhood" (100). This association of "white" and "good" seems to be central to the roles of the characters. A pulsating beat resonates throughout the book,

---

* *This novel was the 1990 winner of Maskew Miller Longman's "Young Africa Series" award.*

but this beat is not identified with the violence committed by the Apartheid system on innocent people. The beat remains neutral. The author takes a noncomittal posture that appears anti–Apartheid, but if Nick, Em, and Theo know anything about the struggle, the author does not tell the reader. Nick's conflict with the mentally disturbed cadet commander has more to do with his girlfriend, Em, and the injury she receives during an antiterrorist school drill than with any new political ideology he has acquired after a two-week interaction with blacks. As a volunteer in a township church, he does have a new experience, but he sums it up as feeling as if he were "in another country."

Who wins in this novel? Nick packs out to stay with Em and her family, but surely he need fear no hassling from the police. The two black youths who found temporary shelter in Nick's home (much to his father's disapproval) and another temporary shelter with Em and Theo—how long will they enjoy this protection? How can white teenagers, still dependent upon their parents, protect the Maphos, Zachs, and other fugitives? How do Nick's problems at home and school relate to the Apartheid situation in which Zach (who ends up in jail) and Mapho find themselves? The only real connection is the budding romance with Em, which has enabled him to meet a new world of people but has not given him time to identify with or accept them. The tiger does not change its spots for want of pride and recognition, for without the spots it is no longer a tiger.

Because of too many hijackings in this novel (too many appropriations of black survival issues by white youngsters) the writer creates a number of disjunctures. However committed some whites were in the anti–Apartheid struggle (and some were indisputably committed), it must not be assumed that Caucasians took the initiative, made the decisions for the blacks, and played the chief roles. Even the white protagonists, who are vividly portrayed by Rosenthal, are left lost in their interactions with their nonwhite associates. In the absence of a dialogue, the setting up of a common strategy and a multiracial platform was squelched before it started. Nick's liberal-minded mother did not have to worry about the fate of the young black fugitives who found temporary refuge in her house. Not one of the liberal whites lost a night's sleep over what was happening to those people whom the author wants the reader to believe are their friends. In short, whites have very little to lose as long as Apartheid takes its time to de-Apartheid itself.

Conclusion

Writing in *The Children's Literature Association Quarterly* in 1988, Carla Hayden and Helen Kay Raseroka note that "the South African situation has unique elements that make it particularly relevant and potentially enthralling in literature for young people of any culture" (57). This observation is very apt. The reality of the drama is that Apartheid is a living organism that daily mortifies blacks—men, women, and children—scarring them physically, mentally, and spiritually. For the literature on this theme to be truly relevant, it must inform and educate. It must expose the reader to the obstacles and explosions that a colonial system inevitably generates. An author's characters and plots should not compromise, marginalize, or trivialize the truth about that system. The outside world has already participated in the Apartheid tragedy by obscuring or distorting vital information. Children's literature, as we see in the novels under discussion here, has been and remains part of that dissembling process.

Works Cited

Achebe, Chinua. *Hopes and Impediments: Selected Essays.* New York: Doubleday, 1989.

Biko, Steve. *I Write What I Like.* (A selection of his writings edited by Aelred Stubbs C.R.) London: Heinemann, 1987. (Originally published in 1978).

Bowen, Elizabeth. *After-Thought: Pieces About Writing.* London: Longman, 1962.

Burt, Struthers. "The Unreality of Realism." In *The Writer and His Craft,* edited by Ray W. Cowden. Ann Arbor: University of Michigan Press, 1954; pp. 191–205.

Gale, Zona. "Writing As Design." In *The Writer and His Craft,* edited by Ray W. Cowden. Ann Arbor: University of Michigan Press, 1954; pp. 30–38.

Hayden, Carla, and Helen Kay Raseroka. "The Good and the Bad: Two Novels of South Africa." *Children's Literature Association Quarterly* 13:1 (Summer, 1988): 57–60.

Rosenthal, Jane. *Wake Up Singing.* Cape Town: Maskew Miller Longman, 1990.

William, Michael. *Crocodile Burning.* New York: Lodestar Books (Dutton), 1992.

Surface and Subliminal Messages

in the Anti–Apartheid Novels of Sheila Gordon and Margaret Sacks

Waiting for the Rain (1987) by Sheila Gordon can best be described as a series of events seen through a misty looking glass. Especially in its depiction of black South African life and its treatment of the 1976 student uprising, this novel is an ambivalent piece of reportage. The book's ambiguities run parallel to the author's ambivalence about the causes and effects of that rebellion—a confrontation between school children and police officers that is symbolized in the lives of the story's two protagonists. As the tale unfolds, it sends distorted images and inaccurate messages about what Apartheid is all about.

The narrative chronicles the lives of Frikkie and Tengo, a white child and a black child born about three months apart. Frikkie is an Afrikaaner, a Boer of Dutch ancestry whose forerunners settled in the Cape around 1652. In particular, Frikkie's family belongs to a group known as Voortrekkers, Boers who migrated to the north after refusing to accept the British law that granted freedom to African slaves. Tengo is a black African whose ethnic connections are not named. He could be Zulu, Xhosa, or one of a number of groups in Southern Africa. Tengo has no impressions of his lineage except what an elder tells him—namely, that "long, long before the kleinbaas's grandfathers came here—long before any white man came here at all—our tribe was here. This was always our land—the land of the tribe" (21).

Trying perhaps to create a multicultural background against which these innocents will grow up as friends, the author establishes many pluses for the white child but a host of minuses for the black African, leaving Tengo with no claim to a land, a culture, or a heritage. Moreover, the so-called friendship is a relationship of child-master and child-servant, and the context of that supposed bond must be understood if the novel's "race problem" is to be honestly dealt with. Before turning to the long range and immediate contexts of the story, we will summarize the plot briefly.

In the first half of the narrative, tension develops from various sources: from the contrasting temperaments of the boys, from their opposite aspirations, and from a political-economic system that is designed to fulfill Frikkie's dreams and squelch Tengo's. Frikkie is known as kleinbaas on his uncle's farm—"little master"—while Tengo is being groomed to become "boss-boy," the top-ranking job in the black population. Frikkie yearns for an end to school days and fulltime life as a farmer; Tengo yearns for an intellectual life and a way to escape the limited and demeaning "boss-boy" existence (the life that is entrapping his father). By delineating the racism that permeates everyday events (e.g., games, parties, farm chores, housing arrangements, etc.), the author attempts to explain why Frikkie has internalized his "master" identity and is not malicious in his indifference toward Tengo's needs and wishes. At the same time, Gordon attempts to establish sympathy for Tengo, but she uses a method that is quite common among white writers—i.e., Tengo is drawn as the one "smart" African in his entire community. He is a gifted sculptor, a quick learner, a companionable playmate, a courageous defender of an African elder's dignity; others in the black group are portrayed as servile, passive, and largely unconcerned about their exploited condition.

After Tengo moves to the city, the novel centers on his new environment—the "good" and "bad" people who are in the midst of the anti–Apartheid struggle. And once Tengo's older cousin, Joseph, gives him an intensive political education, Tengo himself becomes torn between his single-minded pursuit of formal learning and his emerging sense of responsibility toward the struggle for South African democracy. In a street confrontation between army patrolmen and rebelling adolescents, Frikkie-the-soldier and Tengo-the-ambivalent-rebel meet unexpectedly in a shed. Tengo gets the gun, the young men agonize over their past and present fates, and Tengo helps Frikkie escape back to his unit. The sight of Frikkie's blood has convinced him that he must be a revolutionary only from afar; he must go abroad for an education and not join his cousin in an across-the-border guerrilla force. All told, the author informs her readers that anti–Apartheid work must go forward without any internal violence that would impinge on whites. That is the bottom line. If skirmishes with freedom fighters occur at the border, the military can handle that.

You may wonder *how* Tengo can go abroad as a college student given the fact that he lives in devastating poverty. Is he planning to walk to one of those "cold ... and gray" countries where we are told the African National Congress "sends students to school?" Does some sixth sense tell him that he is destined to be one of those "skilled, educated people [needed] when the time comes" (163)? Apparently cousin Joseph is such a topnotch revolutionary that he has good ANC connections, and Tengo is ready to trade on this good luck. Joseph has taken all the risks up to this point, and the inference is that *he* is suited for the blood-spilling part of the struggle because he has never been the bosom pal of a Frikkie, an innocent (albeit benighted) Boer.

Looking at the long-range social context of such a plot, we can identify it as integral to what Anglo-Saxon missionaries and empire-builders were disseminating around the globe. The racial superiority of white over black in Africa, the colonies, and internally in Europe was a myth engrained in Christian teaching and the Christian faith. It then became "scientized" in the pseudosciences of early biologists and anthropologists. Both the religionists and the so-called scientists reinforced an unofficial, but glorified, Apartheid in Europe, Britain, and the Western hemisphere.

But since Gordon's novel deals explicitly with the South African variety of Apartheid, the author provides an immediate context for her tale in the children's rebellion that began on June 16th, 1976. On that day, according to an eyewitness report, "a white policeman in uniform ... pulled out a revolver and aimed it at the pupils standing just in front of him.... [He] fired and more shots followed." A thirteen-year-old was killed, and this started a rebellion that student leaders had attempted to avoid. Knowing that the police were on the way to quell a student march, the leaders told students: "Don't taunt them, don't do anything to them. We are not fighting" (*Weekend World*). The students had been striking Orlando West Junior School for six weeks, but on June 16th the police brought rifles, submachine guns, tear gas, and batons. They did not use their loud hailers to address the students. Said one student: "We thought they were going to disperse us with loud hailers or a loud speaker, or maybe talk to us. But they talked to themselves." Photographer Samuel Nzima of *The World* said later: "The first shot was fired before the children started throwing stones. Then absolute chaos broke out. The children ran all over the place and stoned the police."

While this tragic drama was being played out, whites were in the suburbs, well protected and well provided for. From their safe haven they heard radio and television reports, and a few played the scenario over in their minds until they came up with fictions such as *Waiting for the Rain*.

Gordon chooses to devise a circuitous journey for Frikkie and Tengo and gradually establish a plausible rationale for a close friendship. But the ritual played out in the novel can represent friendship only to those readers who share the same feelings and thoughts as the creator of these fictional boys. There is no real bond. The portraits are skewed as a result of Gordon's white orientation. Her varied cultural innuendos warrant specific interpretation.

Cultures in Contrast

Young Frikkie is understandably fond of his Uncle Oom Koos and his Tant Sannie. They provide a home-away-from-home during school holidays. Frikkie tells his sister, Sissie: "I love the farm, even in winter when everything is dry and brown. I wish I didn't have to go to school. I'd rather be at the farm than anywhere in the world" (2). Additionally, Frikkie will inherit this farm because Oom Koos and Tant Sannie have no children of their own. Throughout the book the reader is given no indication as to why the aunt and uncle remain childless or why they apparently feel no emotion about their childless state. Their infertility is so well-concealed that no signs of psychological or physical strain are in evidence at any time. On the other hand, regarding Tengo's family, the writer lays out for public consumption the alleged faults of black men and women. For example, Selina, Tengo's mother, is stereotyped like most African women as an irresponsible breeder—a woman who keeps breeding even though she has lost two children, a third suffers from tuberculosis, and Tengo cannot be properly provided for. Between Selina and her husband, Timothy, it is implied that they carelessly reproduce without thinking about how the children will be cared for in later life.

Moreover, these parents are portrayed as so intellectually lacking that they fail to question a system that will inevitably thwart their children's prospects. Although Tengo displays a very active, quick mind, the author shows how bleak his chances are because his parents do not have answers to his questions; they have never attempted to answer their own questions or find solutions to their own problems. "His parents went along with the way things were. They asked no questions, and they had no answers when he asked questions" (71-72). Tengo's searching mind never gives up and he asks his father: "'Why can't you have your own farm? Why do you have to work all the time for the oubaas?' His father chuckled. 'A farm costs a lot of money, my boy. Where can a black man get money to buy his own farm'" (72)? It is important to note here that an African father who has been stripped of this dignity as a grownup man would at no time make the mistake of addressing his son as "boy." He would be painfully aware of what "boy" connotes; he is himself labeled "boss-boy." The words of Timothy are merely a white conception of black helplessness. What an African father *would* offer his son in all likelihood would be an African-style maxim that would inform and educate, an aphorism that would help prepare the young man for the future showdown in the struggle for democracy. Or his reply might have been couched in these terms: "*We* don't buy back our own land, land that a stranger-thief has taken by force of the gun."

Words put in the mouth of Tengo's mother are ready-made answers from a white perspective. In his curious way, Tengo queries her about her long workday. "'Mother, how old is the madam?' 'She and I are the same age, Tengo.' 'Then why can't she serve the oubaas his supper and clear the table, so that you could leave earlier and come home and eat supper with us'" (72)? Selina's answer confirms for the reader the preconceived and self-serving opinions of whites. She replies: "Don't ask questions that have no answer, my child. The main thing is to have work and have enough to eat and a place to live with a roof where we can all be together. Nothing else is important" (72).

These exchanges give no indication that indigenous Africans have aspirations and dreams for their children. In the alien names assigned the African characters, there is no hint of African identity, no suggestion of traditional linkages with a culture. In short, no honest effort has been made to lay a baseline of equality or enhance multicultural understanding.

From Tengo's extended family members (his grandmother and the group elder, Ezekial), Tengo hears fragments of information about his culture, but Gordon's misuse of language undermines their significance. For example, Ezekial, an elder in Tengo's community, commends the boy for his skills as a carver and notes that Tengo's grandfather's uncle could "carve figures out of wood, and they were full of life, just as yours are." Unfortunately, Gordon then puts into the mouth of an innocent character a question that one could expect to hear only from a child in the West. Tengo asks, "Did he make toys?" The mask figures that are suggested by the description "full of life" would hardly be mistaken for "toys." They were representatives of the ancestral spirits, intermediaries between the Supreme Being and human beings. They were related to the African concept of God and to the family heritage. This important subject is trivialized further as Ezekial explains that the figures Tengo's forebear carved "were used for magic ceremonies." They "[contained] secrets…. If there was a quarrel with another tribe, he made masks for the men to wear when they danced the dance asking the Gods to secure us the land where we grazed our cattle" (21). The word *magic* would hardly be the proper term for old Ezekiel to use. *Magic* is one of many words of embellishment and misrepresentation used by missionaries in their ridicule of African religious artifacts and ceremonies. These foreigners neither understood nor respected the images they described. The word *secrets* is also misleading, since to the people making use of the image they were not mysterious. Anything looking strange to an outsider in Africa tended to be automatically regarded as "secret."

While the elder *is* sharing cultural information, the looking glass held up by the author is misty. What dance was she referring to when citing the dance "they danced"? Specifics that are of great cultural importance are apparently of little interest to this author.

Various symbolic devices in the novel suggest continuity from one generation to the next, as if a "no future" status for Africans is something that "runs in the blood"! Tengo's Grandma Lettie is forever stirring "a three-legged black iron pot" of white cornmeal porridge. His sister has only one plaything: a carved clay pot and a clay family of figurines carved for her by Tengo. Are we to presume that the child is going to grow up knowing her place? That is, is she part of the next generation that will look after the oubaas and his family? That will breed recklessly like Selina? When Frikkie and Tengo discuss the future, Frikkie is full of pleasant anticipation about his life as master and Tengo's life as servant. At the time of the oubaas's birthday party, Frikkie prattles on and on about the celebration (the barbequed ox, the enormous birthday cake), and then annouces his lifelong plan: "When he dies, this whole farm will be mine. You [Tengo] can work for me and be my boss-boy" (41).

In a word, this supposedly anti–Apartheid novel pretends to expose and condemn all that is evil in Apartheid, yet the narrative includes repeated stereotypes and distortions. There is no suggestion as to how blacks can begin to reconstruct their world and build a positive future for their children. Nowhere is this more evident than in the final sections of the story, scenes that explicitly suggest the maintenance of the status quo.

Sustaining the Status Quo

Incidents and characterizations that are unwittingly pro-Apartheid take various forms in this novel. One form appears in the implication that anarchy will ensue if blacks are not held down. While Gordon does not hesitate to describe police abuses, the most appalling scenes reveal the sadism of young African freedom fighters. For example, at an anti–Apartheid meeting, twelve- and thirteen-year-olds are "discussing putting the 'necklace' on someone." Tengo is striken with horror since the *"necklace* [is] the dreaded punishment inflicted on those considered enemies of the struggle: a tire filled with petrol placed around the victim's neck and set alight" (173). Protesting students are said to resemble "tsotsis," the youthful criminals who terrorize township streets. And girls are letting the school boycotts serve as an excuse for getting pregnant (155).

Another way that Gordon gives support to the status quo is by characterizing blacks as bewildered, indecisive, and unable to cope with new situations and environments. Tengo is depicted as one who is either overwhelmed or incapable of making up his own mind. He breaks up with Emma, his girlfriend, with these words: "It's no use. There is no way we can try to make our lives a little bit better without paying a terrible price" (156). He is shocked to discover that there are black informers everywhere who try to sabotage the anti–Apartheid cause, but he is not impelled to exert any effort on behalf of the prodemocracy movement. He takes direction from the white Methodist minister who tells him: "There are plenty of freedom fighters. There are not that many Tengos. ... Stay with what you've started [that is, formal education]" (148). "Education," as defined by Reverend Gilbert and implicitly by the author, consists of mastering such writers as Shakespeare, Chekov, Camus, and (irony of ironies) Conrad! Among African literary critics, the novel, *Heart of Darkness*, firmly situates Conrad among colonialist writers. Chinua Acheba explains the chief issue when he analyzes Conrad as one of those "liberals" of his times who "always managed to sidestep the ultimate question of equality between white people and black people" (Acheba, 10).

This sidestepping aptly describes what Gordon does when she shows Tengo's friend Bennie as unable to deal with changes in his environment. He has abandoned his studies in a northern European country because of cold weather, loneliness, and his discomfort in the midst of people with a different language. "He couldn't sleep. He began to have nightmares.

... He thought he would go mad if he didn't see the sun" (172). If such superficial changes induce madness, how can blacks endure the transition to a new political system? Africans, to the colonialist mind, are frozen in time and not psychologically stable enough to endure social change. It is hard to imagine the novelist characterizing Europeans with Bennie's emotional fragility.

While undoubtedly opposed to the following educational platform of the Apartheid government, Gordon sends subliminal messages that suggest a degree of consent. That platform was summed up in 1954 by the Minister of Native Affairs: "When I have control of native education, I will reform it so that the natives will be taught from childhood to realize that equality with Europeans is not for them.... What is the use of teaching the Bantu child mathematics when it cannot use it in practice? That is quite absurd." Tengo, at the end of the novel, is about to follow in Bennie's footsteps. Will an adventure in learning on foreign soil cause a similar destablizing effect?

Finally, in the scene in which Tengo wounds Frikkie and takes away his gun, the author instills fear and suspicion in the minds of Western children who are more and more surrounded by guns. The image of Frikkie in his military uniform, performing his duties as a soldier, conjures in Western thought less anxiety than an armed black man. Although Tengo uses the occasion to merely pour out his grievances to his bewildered childhood acquaintance, this choice only tempers slightly the vocabulary of colonialism that other parts of the novel articulate.

For another ambivalent anti–Apartheid message and an even more explicit statement about the dangers of black African activism, we turn to Margaret Sacks' *Beyond Safe Boundaries*. As a parable that becomes transfigured into a paradox, the novel denies that there are any "safe boundaries" anywhere.

Beyond Safe Boundaries

Margaret Sacks probably intends in this novel to put on display the younger generation's advances beyond neocolonialism. However, she frequently contradicts this idea of progress, as when the protagonist's father becomes the voice of "realism" and explains what can be expected from the black revolutionary. He instructs the novel's fourteen-year-old narrator:

> "There is room in this country for only two types of people: Those who believe in the system, and those who passively abide by it."
>
> "But what about those who are willing to fight?" I ventured. ...
>
> "Haven't you seen enough to know the answer to that question? ... Dying or being imprisoned for your ideals won't change a thing, and the black man won't even thank you for it. One day, when Lena's [the maid's] son returns like a mindless fighting machine and you are standing in his path, he's not going to know that you are the white girl his mother loves like her own daughter. Nor is he going to stop and think, Ah, let's spare this one, she truly has a good heart" [154–55].

This discussion occurs at the end of the novel and allows the adolescent to make a rite-of-passage gesture, to distance herself from her father's conviction that exile is her only option. She vows to fight the system with words. The irony is that Sacks' words present the novel's population of blacks in largely demeaning terms.

In a gossipy-cum-reminiscent narrative, Sacks paints a colorful montage of the home and school encounters of two sisters. She invites her readers into the home of Dr. Levins (a dentist), his daughters, his new wife, and his array of black African servants. This is a Jewish family that knows the pain of ethnic discrimination. The young narrator, Elizabeth, explains: "My father was ... a golf enthusiast, but he wasn't allowed to be a member of the club across the road for the same reason I'd been refused admission to the Port Elizabeth Municipal Tennis Club when I was nine years old: No Jews allowed" (7). But a Jewish heritage does not exclude the Levin family from the "white" side of the racial fence. The doctor practices his profession without interference or harassment from the Apartheid police. His youngest child goes to that "bastion of the British Empire, Queen Victoria Junior School for [white] Girls" (3). Elizabeth, the narrator-cum-protagonist, describes with sardonic humor her life in this snooty school, plus the personal affairs of everyone in the neighborhood. But in addressing the minor characters (mainly an indigenous and mixed race group), the young narrator puts on display their questionable characters, behaviors, and peculiarities.

Elizabeth pinpoints the day when her "world began to unsettle" as the day her father's new bride moved in. But using such a symbol vis-à-vis life in South Africa hardly does justice to the sensitive issues of the 1950s. The loss and replacement of a mother was unquestionably traumatic, but it hardly compares with the dangerous conditions to which a black child was exposed in that era. Aside from this weak starting focus, Sacks' use of a naive narrator works against the professed anti–Apartheid

ould think that such an innocent as Elizabeth would be
ith the multiracial mix that surrounds her, especially since
ly confronts irrational discrimination. But this does not
he case. The girl's disparaging remarks and descriptions of
blacks make her a party to the usual white-on-black racism of the
Apartheid system. In short, the author's use of a Jewish family setting as
a way to reinforce the anti–Apartheid theme proves counterproductive;
the family's response to "things not English" swings between open insult
and undisguised disdain. What is important to understand here is that
while the offensive racist behavior of the naive narrator constitutes part
of her characterization, the novelist's voice should not be in concurrence.
In her depiction of blacks, the novelist must somehow hint at an alternative viewpoint. To plausibly communicate an anti–Apartheid stance,
Sacks must not undermine her audience's faith in black rule. But Sacks'
Africans (with the exception of her token martyr) range from the
degraded, to the ridiculous, to the sinister.

Contradictions in Black Characterization

First, Mr. Coetzee (derisively nicknamed "Popeye") is treated as brilliant
in his trade, but he is so saddened by the fact that he "lacks an identity"
that he takes to drink. He is Dr. Levin's dental mechanic, and although
the doctor puts himself at risk by hiring a "colored" in a nonmenial job,
it is the doctor who sees him as devoid of identity because he is a mixed-
race South African. Both the author and the narrator view Mr. Coetzee
with some sympathy (we are told that he would have made a "brilliant
dentist"), but the usual trademark innuendos are fastened on him: a drinking problem and "unusual circumstances [in] his personal life" (48). The
"unusual circumstances" refer to the fact that his wife is white, his son
passes for white, they live in an all-white neighborhood, and Mr. Coetzee is essentially homeless. He stumbles through the novel with increasingly bloodshot eyes. At no point does the writer put the blame where it
squarely belongs—on the fascist system that will eventually cause the
murder of his son and his own suicide.

Beauty is another example of how an insistent degradation warps a
promising African's destiny. Beauty wants to work with her Aunt Lena in
the Levin household, and after much hustling on Lena's part, she is hired
as a new maid. At this point the author chooses to express a truly hateful

attitude toward a black woman. She has Elizabeth and her friend invite Beauty to dance and describes her motions derisively: "her head jerked back and forth like an inquisitive chicken's" (64). She ridicules her alleged fleshiness: "[Beauty's] heavy, swaying breasts and buttocks ... rose and fell in a rhythm special only to African women..." (63). On another occasion Beauty needs no encouragement when asked to dance a topless dance for the girls and for the young man next door who has planted himself at the window. Sacks describes her with such terms as "sensuous," "voluptuous," and "gyrating"—apparently in preparation for the scenes in which Beauty will invite tsotsis (young criminals) to her room and become sluggish, fat, and pregnant.

Both Lena and the cook, Mathilda, are alternately portrayed as ridiculous and corrupt. It is hard to believe that the stereotypic black "comic" is presented to readers as harmless humor: "'*Hayi, hayi, hayi!*' Mathilda clapped her hands... 'What you do?' she asked, pulling at my chopped-up hair. 'You plucked chicken or what! And Miss Evie, she going to be mad hatter with you'" (11). Elizabeth then notes for the reader that Tilly's "vocabulary had become more colorful since I had read her excerpts from *Alice in Wonderland*." Elizabeth's scorn takes various forms, as when she mimics Mathilda's "*yo! yo! yo!*" "Her laugh was an expulsion of air through the gaps between her long, yellow teeth and sounded like the water draining out of our bathtub. I copied her, which I knew she found irritating" (12). While Lena and Mathilda both "yo, yo, yo" their way through the book, they also break things out of clumsiness and ignorance, create an environment of squalor in their sleeping quarters, practice foolish-sounding religious taboos, leave their jobs without notice, gossip for hours on the phone unless under constant surveillance, tell lies—in short, Sacks takes every opportunity to validate the fears and angers of white South Africans vis-à-vis their servants. Attention is consciously diverted from the horrors blacks endure under Apartheid; instead, white guilt is replaced with black guilt.

The texture of the novel is woven with these everyday encounters between "masters" and servants. Plot action takes a noticeable anti–Apartheid turn when Wilhelm, Mr. Coetzee's son, is arrested and then pushed from a police station window. He has predicted that this will be his fate if he is caught for his role in antigovernment agitation. Evie, Elizabeth's older sister, has become a student revolutionary in the midst of black, colored, and Indian comrades. Evie has become suddenly aware of the dynamics between "master" and servant, and her protests within the

Movement will eventually cause her incarceration under "house arrest." But the novel remains essentially Elizabeth's coming-of-age drama, and when Evie hints that she may well be kicked out of the nest if a baby is born to her stepmother, the anxiety she feels becomes an analogue for what South African whites fear from black rule.

Conclusion

The ambivalence toward Apartheid in the Gordon and Sacks novels places these writers well within Western traditions and cultural norms. The plots encompass protest, while the texture of the works is cautious and in some instances even retrogressive. Both Tengo and Lena's son become involved in the "freedom" movement. Both are sons of black maids. The white men, Oom Koos and Dr. Levin, fail to understand that the system they support (the system that is supporting *them*) has been established by ruthlessly destroying the prospects of black and mixed-race children. Indeed, these children have been write-offs from the outset—disadvantaged at birth and destined for the white establishment's menial jobs.

Critics who probably see themselves within a "liberal" tradition nonetheless lend support to the colonial myth of superiority by heaping praises and prizes upon *Waiting for the Rain* and *Beyond Safe Boundaries*. By elevating these works to "best book" status, the process of perpetuating white power gains reinforcement. And with these two books there has hardly been a dissenting voice. *Waiting for the Rain* received the Jane Addams award, a prize commending the book for its contribution to peace in the world. It has been included as a best book about friendship in *Booklist*'s "Growing Up Male" bibliography. The "Young Adult Editors' Choice" books for 1989 include *Beyond Safe Boundaries*, and the annotation refers to the work as a "powerful story that raises questions about political responsibility" (995). *Social Education* calls Sacks' book "outstanding" (87). *The Book Report* urges Sacks to "continue her fight, as Elizabeth vows, 'with words'" (47).

Apartheid began to crumble because the international world could not forever turn a blind eye to another Nazism. The question we must ask is whether the antifascist message is accompanied by another message in these novels: by Western fears and suspicions that are being passed along because such distrusts remain central in each author's thoughts.

Works Cited

Achebe, Chinua. *Hopes and Impediments: Selected Essays.* New York: Doubleday, 1989.

Brook, Diane L., Linda D. Labbo, and Sherry L. Field. Rev. of *Beyond Safe Boundaries* by Margaret Sacks in "The Peaceful Revolution: Some Teaching Resources." *Social Education* 59:2 (Feb. 1995): 87.

Burbridge, Carol A. Rev. of *Beyond Safe Boundaries* by Margaret Sacks. *Book Report* 8:3 (Nov./Dec., 1989): 47.

Gordon, Sheila. *Waiting for the Rain: A Novel of South Africa.* New York: Orchard Books (Franklin Watts), 1987.

Rochman, Hazel and Stephanie Zvirin. Rev. of *Waiting for the Rain: A Novel of South Africa* in "Growing Up Male: Friends." *Booklist* 90:3 (Oct. 1, 1993): 334.

Sacks, Margaret. *Beyond Safe Boundaries.* New York: Dutton, 1989.

"Young Adult Editors' Choice." Rev. of *Beyond Safe Boundaries* by Margaret Sacks. *Booklist* 86:10 (Jan. 15, 1990): 1992.

Envisioning
a New South Africa

Mixed Signals in Novels and Scholarship

Fiction writers as well as scholars are foreseeing a new social and political life for South Africa. As seers, both groups can fulfill a vital artistic function. To refashion an imaginative landscape can lead the way in refashioning a literal one. As the novelist lets imagination take a daring leap, the reader follows with a willing suspension of disbelief. And the literary critic contributes a sensibility that magnifies the work's values, while sharpening its outlines. But the challenge for both artist and critic is the challenge of consistency. The objects of their praise must conform to their professed idealism.

In Ann Harries' *The Sound of the Gora* (1980) and Janet Smith's *Streams to Rivers* (1988) there is a noticeable discrepancy between vision and achievement. And in Andree-Jeanne Totemeyer's critiques of these works, there is more wishful thinking about "common southern African culture identity" than a convincing demonstration of common ground. Admittedly, Totemeyer cautions that "there is still a long way to go" (15). However, this scholar's claim that African mythology is "fused with Western and other values and internalized by young literary characters irrespective of race" is at best, we would argue, a half-truth. Moreover, in her critique of a poetry anthology, Totemeyer observes that "the collection succeeds in bringing together mythological beliefs from various cultures without emphasizing or even mentioning the origins of each, resulting in a dynamic creation which will stimulate and be recognized by all children from southern Africa" (14). This applause for cultural anonymity undercuts the quality that gives South Africa its national uniqueness. To erase the distinct sources of mythological beliefs is to deprive the myths themselves of their right of origin; it denies specific peoples their right of ownership. This lumping together follows the usual pattern of overgeneralization in discussions of Africa.

Cultural identity has not been stripped from the well known European classics. Hans Christian Andersen's work is infused with the elements of Nordic culture, yet his stories transcend their linguistic and cultural boundaries. And the same can be said for the tales of the Brothers Grimm. One reason such works have survived is their faithful preservation of cultural identity.

Turning to the discussion of novels, Totemeyer explains that "the literary function of the mythological element in [*The Sound of the Gora*] is to act as an agent of cohesion, as a dynamic healing force in a racially divided South Africa" (15). This is a questionable assertion; one must ask whether the mythologies have suddenly become understood by writers whose forebears were bent on annihilating Africans and their cultures. How can these "mythological elements" act as agents of cohesion when they have been taken out of context, their very origins obscured? In a racially divided society, it is necessary to go to the very root causes of the racial divide. To capitalize on elements of the oppressed culture and still expect to get a healing result is to paper over the deep-seated scars and unhealed wounds inflicted by the colonizer. It is to evade the colonial dynamic. Sociologist Stephen Small writes that "[whites] demarcated the acceptable terrain (political, economic, social) which could be traversed by black people, while keeping all terrains open to non-blacks" (15). This point needs to remain in the foreground as both *The Sound of the Gora* and *Streams to Rivers* are examined. While African myths are alluded to in these novels of modern life, the color line is firmly in place in both works.

The Sound of the Gora

Ann Harries' novel shifts alternately between two time frames: 1800 and 1976. In the 1800s, the Boers hunted down and annihilated the Bushmen, at the same time entrapping their children and selling them as slaves to the British. In 1976, there was open confrontation in the form of strikes and street demonstrations between the Apartheid (Boer) system and the blacks (which included the coloreds* and other nonwhite groups). The

---

*The coloreds (by South African definition) are the product of cohabitation between Europeans and Africans. They are defined as "the people who do not look like or are not accepted as being white or African. ... [T]hey are generally lighter skinned than Africans, but darker than whites." They number approximately two and a half million in South Africa. (See Hirson, p. 216.)

author uses flashbacks to create continuity and link past and present traditionally and culturally. She also uses an ancient stringed instrument, the gora, as a device to unite Bushman ancestral spirits with their living descendants.

Harries' main focus is on the colored community, the in-between group once pronounced as a "statutory category" only. (Under Apartheid laws they were declared a nation but a nation without a "homeland.") From this background we encounter Andre, the protagonist of the 1976 time frame. Readers travel with this colored boy into the past and follow in the journey that will reunite him with his Bushman father. Andre believes himself orphaned, since he lives with his grandmother and since neighbors have informed him of the murder of his father by the criminal who later became his deceased mother's lover.

A secondary plotline involves Caroline, who believes herself to be white and lives in a posh all-white suburb. Her father has never informed her that her mother was a colored-passing-for-white, that her sister, Naomi, was shunted off to live with her grandparents at birth, and that her mother (now exposed as a fraud and law-breaker) died of a broken heart. Caroline will ultimately discover and join forces with Naomi.

African mythology in this tale relates to the gora (whose sounds can reconcile) and the story of the Mantis and the Hartebeest (a Bushman folktale). No one except Andre and Caroline can hear the gora music, and they are bonded together because of it. The folktale is used symbolically for its theme about wholeness and cohesion. In the tale, Bushman children cut up a dead hartebeest, but discover that it is really Father Mantis dressed in the body of the animal. Magically, the various parts of the carcass spring together and the "Mantis in the Hartebeest's body stood before them, whole, and without any wounds" (89). Totemeyer makes much of this symbolism, seeing the reunions in the novel as representative of Apartheid's demise.

However, the overall sentiments in this novel do not come naturally from the characters. The vibrations coming from the gora have a mystery for which the protagonists are not culturally equipped to understand. How much of the animist religious life do the children who follow "the Gora" know? There is no evidence of an African spiritual connection that could inspire "magic" or bring together children in a society where neither of the twain are allowed to meet. They journey to a plateau of rock and an "ancient tree, with its mass of coiled roots hunched like talons beneath its trunk" (65), but even if they have discovered ancestor spirits dwelling in the tree, are they prepared to make the necessary sacrifices? And what would those sacrifices be? For it is not just hearing the sound and following it that matters; rather it is performing the ritual that will ultimately shape and influence their actions. If Andre and Caroline are to prepare for the Mantis/Hartebeest union, they must share the experience like twins, not as one humiliated colored child in the presence of one curious white onlooker. The spirit world of the African tradition is not just freakish mythology. But how much of this is understood by Western writers who try to introduce the indigenous traditions in their writings? Harries had experience as a teacher in nonwhite schools, but she presents the characters in the novel as victimized by their own actions rather than by a system that has preordained the outcome for those born of the "wrong" color. She poses as an anti–Apartheid storyteller but places her concentration upon colored-on-colored violence. That makes Apartheid appear a means of protecting law-abiding whites from a corrupted community of blacks. In the student rebellion scenes, police officers do crack youthful skulls, but this violence hardly compares with the horrors of daily life in Andre's neighborhood. And the overlap that Harries creates between anti–Apartheid protesters and vicious delinquents results in an essentially pro–Apartheid statement. Specific examples make the point.

Rebels and Felons

Student protesters (led by Andre's seventeen-year-old friend, Yusuf) are largely portrayed as too immature to spearhead a social movement. The reader is invited to witness one boycott planning meeting in which Yusuf and his associates discuss violent versus nonviolent action. Yusuf wants to avoid elitism and create a mass movement, but by inviting "skollies" (the colored equivalents of "tsotis," young criminals), he weakens his leadership role. The "skollies" advocate killing rather than being killed, and in trying to out-shout them, Yusuf shames them by charging them with cowardice. They kill blacks only, he says, just as the white police hope they will. This exchange turns the meeting into a brawl, but its effect is to make this gang taunt and stab a young white man waiting for a bus. Not only is Yusuf depicted as a Communist (validating the accusation directed at dissidents by pro–Apartheid forces); he is also someone who is incapable of wisely leading his peers.

Yusuf is well-intentioned but not a key player in this drama. The novelist devotes most of her space to instances of black sadism and moral weakness. Ringo, for example, is the killer who has fathered Andre's two half-sisters. He "chopped [Andre's father] with his butterfly axe, and left him dead on the pavement. Then he cut out his eye to prove it" (25). He lives with Andre's mother after that and she becomes a drunk and a prostitute. Andre, says the narrator, is able to blot out the "bad bits" about his mother—"the drunken screams, the vomiting, the other men who would burst into Ouma's [the grandmother's] room and pull out chunks of his mommy's hair before his very eyes" (26). Ringo's behavior is not an isolated case. His gang participates in axing anyone in their path ("Chop! down he goes, lucky if they leave him with his ears and nose to say nothing of his head") (24).

While this local terrorism is going on, the citizenry play cards, smoke pot, guzzle liquor, and ridicule student protesters:

> The card parties outside Somerset House [the decaying tenement where Andre lives] had already started by the time Andre got home…. Mr. Japie from down the road carefully placed the half full bottle under the table, so as not to tempt onlookers…. Mr. January, of no fixed abode, dealt his hand triumphantly and reached under the table to celebrate.
> Mr. Kleintjies from upstairs lifted his hat with mock respect to Andre. "Good evening my friend. And can you tell me how the revolution's coming on?"
> "Black is beautiful, hey Andre?" called out Mr. October. "I'll drink to that…" [36–37].

This is one of several repartees in which colored adults mock such concepts as "Black Power," "Black Consciousness," and the idea that "Black-is-Beautiful." Both adults and children smoke marijuana incessantly. The nightwatchman at the factory that Andre and his peers are burglarizing is in a drug-induced stupor. He is jarred awake by a wailing sound that he interprets as witchcraft. The novelist makes this character and his beliefs in the supernatural as disgusting as possible:

> Frantically the old man began unbuttoning his flies. There is only one way to counteract the ill-effects of the Tokolosh [an evil spirit]: had not his own father saved his life by this very method when he lay groaning with sickness in the smoky kraal?
> As the water splashed against the wall, the would-be robbers dispersed as rapidly as they had appeared [46].

Descriptions of coloreds remain at this cheap, crude level throughout the book, whether the portrait is of Andre's grandmother, Yusuf's mother, or the varied male loiterers who populate the story. No adult coloreds are portrayed as worthy individuals with the exception of Dixu, Andre's father, who appears as a shadowy figure at the end of the novel, a man living out his days in a pitch-black cave. (He has recovered from Ringo's assault but is missing one eye.) In short, the scenario designated as a "1976" drama would hardly lead one to believe in democracy (in this case, black rule) rather than the minority rule of whites. For instead of talking about the twentieth-century rape of Africa's wealth and labor, this novel's concern is hooliganism and colored-on-colored atrocities.

In the "1800" drama, the cultural/political inferences are also questionable. Harries reveals the total dispossession of African land and liberty resulting from European incursions, but the Africans' response is barely understood and often misrepresented.

The Initial Dutch/Bushman Encounters

In 1800, young Andre Pretorius goes with his father and other Boer farmers on a commando-style massacre of the Bushmen people. The child's task was to encourage Korel, the Bushman chief, to surrender:

> You will get safe conduct if only you take my hand. My father says I am to tell you once more, for the last time, that your tribe will be saved if you surrender now... I have pleaded with my father on your behalf. He has told the commando to stay their guns if you will come with me. Take my hand. I will be your shield [14].

Andre's entreaties sound sincere, but Korel is aware that Andre is only a child and a messenger. The lives and freedom of his people could not be entrusted to the gesture of locking hands with a young boy—a youngster who has yet to understand that "the frog does not entertain the snake to dinner and expect to go free." Korel knows that he cannot depend on the promises of people whose interests involve deception and destruction. He replies to Andre: "Go! Be gone! Tell your father that I am not a child. ... Be gone! My eyes cannot bear the sight of you any longer.... Tell your father ... that I shall resist and defend myself as long as I have life left!" (15).

It seems that only the whites in South Africa could not understand that anger against them had never been far below the surface from the day they set foot on the Cape. Korel's daughter, Nama, watches the slaying of her parents and the rest of her community from behind a rock, but her anger is treated superficially. In fact, she falls madly in love with the Andre who took part in the fatal confrontation. Nama is initially to be sold with the other children to British slavers, but instead Andre's mother decides to train her as a household servant. Mrs. Pretorius orders her Hottentot servant: "Pick her up, Tomorrow, let's take her inside and clean off her Bushman filth" (30).

Nama is renamed Marguerite, learns to read with the help of Andre, and attends the prayer meetings conducted for the whole household by Mr. Pretorius. The patriarch prays for forgiveness in conjunction with prayers for power over the land, the Bushmen, and the so-called "Kaffirs." He calls Bushmen "Little Yellow Vermin" and tells the gathering that "The Lord God is with us.... In his Holy Book we read clearly what we are to do.... There were some that he made masters, and some that he made servants.... The Lord God Himself has ordained that each man shall know his place" (68, 70). The author informs us that Nama is so lovesick she cannot even glance at Andre: Nama "was struggling with a surge of love that threatened to choke her as she strangled it. She must not look at him, or that love would flood out through her eyes" (66). Why does she feel so strongly for the son of the man who has made her an orphan? Who ordered the slaughter of her family? Who insults her people? Who sold her brother into slavery?

As for the Andre of the 1800 flashback, he is cautious about his emotions for Nama, if he has any. His characterization is very low-keyed. There is no indication that he questions the religious myth that God led his "chosen people" to South Africa to fulfill an ordained purpose. Surely the Dutch settlers found that the Bushmen had their own way of worship, their own God (gods). But the Pretorius family conveniently interprets its own holy text in ways that justify disrespect for African religion.

Like the coloreds in the 1976 scenario, Nama is awed and enamoured by whites. The skollies kill their own neighbors but will not confront a white person until provoked by Yusuf, the resistance leader. Nama has such a passion it almost "chokes" her. What is the attraction? How can people make themselves an easy prey to predator-settlers?

Harries sets up this Nama/Andre romance as an element of hope even within the slave context of the early nineteenth century. This is a doubtful "reading" of the nineteenth century, but she does outline the severe oppression of the times and thereby establishes an anti–Apartheid theme. Then her treatment of the 1970s contradicts that theme because her approach is ahistorical. She omits the important relationship between the

1970s student movement and the reenergized labor movement in South Africa. This is pertinent to this novel because Harries could have portrayed the 1970s colored and black adults in a manner commensurate with their actual historical importance. Instead, she turns both young and old into deadbeats.

The Historical Context of the Student Movement

Steve Biko, the African martyr of the 1970s, stated in regard to the student movement that young people felt duty-bound to play the role that they were capable of playing. He said that "the primary reason behind the unrest is simple lack of patience by the young folk with a government which is refusing to change, refusing the change in the educational sphere, which is where they [the students] are directing themselves, and also refusing to change in a broader political situation" (147). Labor strikes had been leading the way and students needed to be similarly active in their own sphere.

In Namibia in 1971, 12,000 workers from tin, copper, lead, and zinc mines went on strike against a contract system that was almost slave-like (workers could not choose their employers; they could not live with their families; they could not strike; they could not resign since the contract designated a fixed period of employment; they could not easily live on the low wages) (Hirson, 131). The "message" sent by this strike spurred renewed labor unrest in South Africa, and 200,000 blacks were on strike between 1973 and 1976. The Natal University Social Research Department reported in 1970 that 85 percent of African families in the industrial complex of Durban lived in poverty (Hirson, 131, 133). Obviously the workers had no savings and could not sustain a long-term strike that would carry real clout. Additionally, since army trainees filled in as "scabs," the economic effects of the strikes were minimal. There was little strikers could do to alter the oppressive labor conditions (e.g., the wages for white miners in 1972 was 391 rand per month in contrast to 24 rand for Africans—a 15:1 ratio) (Hirson, 147). Moreover, strikers could not formally organize because once the leadership became known, the government jailed or drove out the leaders. Given these conditions, a worker-student joint effort was not possible. But students realized their unique ability to carry out a prolonged boycott and took advantage of this leverage.

The point of recording this background information here is simply to suggest that the slanderous treatment of the adult community in *The

Sound of the Gora is baffling as well as unconscionable. Elders as well as young people were part of the prodemocracy struggle. The atmosphere of revolt established by workers set the precedent for political revolt on a larger scale.

The catalyst that served to unite both primary and secondary school dissidents was the government's requirement that Afrikaans rather than English be the language of instruction. This move by the authorities was a divide-and-conquer strategy, as the students were well aware. English, not Afrikaans, was the language that bound blacks in urban areas together; it was the language of the international community. Moreover, the switch to Afrikaans was a means of creating a more entrenched economic underdevelopment for blacks, since English was the language of industry and commerce.

The sophistication of students vis-à-vis their own condition is a feature noticeably lacking in the novels about the school boycotts. Nor is the range of political activity alluded to. Parents sometimes joined the youngsters. Teachers and students conducted teach-ins. Martin Luther King Jr.'s leadership and agenda were studied (Hirson, 177, 178). At the University of Witwatersrand, 400 white students joined in the marching as a gesture of support (Hirson, 185). But the most serious omission in *The Sound of the Gora* is the failure to even hint at the actual degree of suffering. What were the students in Woodstock so riled about? They had learned of Soweto: 96 had died and over 1000 had been injured in three days; hospitals and mortuaries were made inaccessible to parents and relatives; injured students were denied treatment until police officers had examined them (Hirson, 187).

When *The Sound of the Gora* was published in 1980, government officials may have worried about the coverage of student protests, since they banned the book. But on reflection they apparently decided that "the system" was safe in Harries' hands and the novel was no longer banned. Blacks are demeaned in the story to the degree that Apartheid ("separate development") looks rational. Professor Totemeyer has called the novel "a dynamic healing force in a racially divided South Africa of the seventies" (15), but we would argue that the crafting of the novel sends a very mixed message.

The Question of Craft

The symbols and images in this story are heavily biased towards a partial-white unity, a highly selective multiracial togetherness. The tying of the pieces together does not positively bring the rejects, the deprived and the rich in all their various colors under one umbrella. They are not all to be protected from the storm that precedes a "new dawn." Nama is the ancestral mother of Andre-the-colored-boy; she is the child reborn in Naomi, the half-colored sister of Caroline. Nama had to travel to the unknown in search of her enslaved brother; Naomi lives in the racially demarcated zone of a town in Cape Province. Have the circumstances improved for Nama's descendants? The folktale is alluded to with the words, "the Mantis will answer your prayer," but how long has it taken for this voice to start whispering that there is hope for all? This novel, as a whole, smacks of "light-skinned" fraternity. The symbolic powers of the Mantis and the Hartebeest do not extend to the Muslims (Mrs. Ibrahim and her son Yusuf); the music of the gora does not reach the colored winos who are equally the descendants of Nama, the mother-ancestor.

In trying to piece together where this novel is headed and what avenues are open for achieving a "new dawn," one realizes that the voice of the old Boer is transferred to the skollie who randomly stabs a white student and mumbles: "We don't like your face" (107). That Boer voice was the Bible-reading voice of the 1800s. In the knife-wielding boy is the spirit of the ancestor who is not ready to move on after four hundred and more years of lies and crimes, inhuman acts committed in the name of the "One God." Regardless of race, religious persuasion, or gender, people have been striving throughout time to know this deity as best they can.

Whether crafting or studying *The Sound of Gora*, the reinstalling of Africa within "the equalities of world consciousness" is a necessary premise. Chinua Achebe makes the point:

> Certainly anyone, white or black, who chooses to see violence as the abiding principle of African civilization is free to do so. But let him not pass himself [herself] off as a restorer of dignity to Africa, or attempt to make out that he [or she] is writing about ... the state of civilization in general [80].

Streams to Rivers

A second novel commended for its "common southern African culture identity" is Janet Smith's *Streams to Rivers*, a strange, hither-thither romance involving Michelle (a white girl), Walter (a Zulu boy), and Gavin (a white boy). At the center is Michelle, whose mother has died by the bullet of a poacher. Michelle, we are told, has all the attributes of her mother, including beauty, an open-mindedness toward blacks, and an affection for them. Michelle's father explains to her: "'I love you Micky, but you're too much like your mother was. She—' and he ended suddenly and looked out the window" (24). Michelle asks him to continue, but his sudden hesitation suggests that there are details he wishes to conceal.

In fact, Michelle's mother had been planning to go away with an African anthropologist, a man she had fallen in love with while attending the university. Her sudden abandonment of this plan leads one to suspect that she was going in for an unchristian-like setup which involved poligamy (although this explanation is omitted from the novel). Dad continues his circumspect discussion with his daughter:

> She wanted to take you to Swaziland with her just before the accident with the poacher. She wanted to go and live there with her friends, her black friends. She knew a family there ... and they had small children of your age at that time, seven years old, or so. Your mom wanted to bring you up with those people, so that you wouldn't grow up believing that you are better than them, or that they were different from you [24].

After the death of Michelle's mother, Pauline, the black maid/housekeeper/cook/nanny became like a mother to Michelle. However, whether the motherless girl wanted to believe it or not, Pauline was different in a special way. Like other blacks of her status, she was treated differently by Michelle's father, who dined with Mercedes-owning blacks but made Pauline drink from her own special cup as a precaution against contamination.

The romance develops between Michelle and Pauline's grandson, Walter, after he helps Michelle with an assignment about consciousness-raising and is later implicated in the accident that leaves the girl temporarily confined to a wheel chair. The incident occurs when Walter's understandable anger comes into the open:

> "Come outside. I have something to show you," he'd demanded, and ... he grabbed her hand roughly and pulled her towards the back fence.... A very tall, fat white man was standing over a crouching black man, wielding a plank above his head. The plank already seemed to be stained with brown blood [10].

The grisly beating continues with Walter shouting to Michelle: "Look! Look at this! Your project did not include this man! ... How many times has this happened and you didn't even know? He is the man you and your friends do not know!" (11). Why does not Walter, Michelle, or a white onlooker call the police? As the story progresses, nothing more is said about the black man who was being beaten to death. The shock, the accident (Michelle has fled from the scene and been struck by a car), and Michelle's paralysis are the images representing pain.

But the accident, we are told, has created a bond between the young people, while it also separates Michelle from her family and peers. Smith writes about this separation throughout her novel, revealing different degrees of racism in the protagonist's circle of friends. These responses to a Caucasian/black union serve to highlight the book's anti–Apartheid theme, but at the same time the author develops scenes that cloud an African perspective.

A Spectrum of Response

Approaching Africa for its exciting "exoticness" is a common means of trivializing unfamiliar traditions. Smith takes the novel down that path when she introduces Gavin, another potential boyfriend for the protagonist. Gavin's home is full of photographs that introduce Michelle to Zimbabwe and West Africa. She is taken on a vicarious tour by way of an interior decorator's collection of nameless masks with real hair. Whatever these masks symbolize, or whatever they mean to the people to which they originally belonged, this, it seems, is of no consequence.

In another encounter, Michelle meets her father's friend, Father Thomas, a retired priest. Father Thomas recounts his blissful experiences in a mission in Lesotho, describing for Michelle a "special love":

> ...we loved each other, and it was a special kind of love, a love that we shared with the students in our little school, and the young mothers who came to us for guidance, and the older folk who came for meals and to talk. That is the marvelous thing about being fortunate enough to speak an African language. The things these old people spoke about cannot be translated into English or Afrikaans or any other language. These old people were wise, and what they said made wonderful sense, even though they used many proverbs and natural descriptions [32].

Surely, if readers are to understand the twists and turns on the one-way street Smith is driving up, they must not be fed images that do not help them think things out. Why does she imply that it is difficult for Western audiences to comprehend simple African proverbs? And what is she trying to communicate with the priest's reference to "natural descriptions"? In even the remotest villages in Africa, Euro-American pop culture, gang culture, bomb culture, and other flourishing Western styles are known and discussed. Why the notion of mysterious or dense indigenous thought? Father Thomas should have been able to elucidate those "natural descriptions," which, being "natural," must transcend language and color barriers. All told, the suggestion here is that a hiatus exists—a suspension in time and meaning—rather than a basis for intercultural cohesion.

Another problematic character is Pauline-the-maid, who dies before the novel's finale. With her last dying breath she tells Walter: "'Go to the hills Mandlenkosi, and take Michelle as a woman. Take her and show her...'" (77). What should Walter show Michelle? Why should he wait until she is a woman (she understands that she is already getting there)? And why Michelle? Is she to complete what her mother failed to accomplish? The reader knows by now that no one in Michelle's camp will accept the friendly relationship between these young people. How is it that Pauline could look upon her adored grandson and wish to sacrifice him to a hostile environment? An environment that denied her even the most elementary human rights?

Pauline represents the neocolonialist theme that presents so-called "inferiors" as ready to give their lives or take risks for the supposed "superiors." The "contented slave" has a devotion to the enslaver that knows no bounds. Also Pauline represents the neocolonialist logic that "primitives" are destined for a life of subservience. She is treated as if she is born to servitude because she "seemed, somehow, to breathe the air of an earlier time" (28). Has her contact with colonial Africa predisposed her in some mysterious way to menial work? When she is so frail and ill that she can hardly hold the broom, she remains cheerfully at work. And no one offers to help, no one suggests that she go into retirement, no one takes her to the hospital. We are told that after leaving her birthplace as a young woman she became disenchanted with urban life and the role of a perpetual work-horse. But she was not able to return home because her family was (and is) so intolerant that they exiled her permanently. Even when she is ill she insists that her family will not allow her grandson to visit her because "they would say that she had chosen to come to the city and that she was being punished by the spirits for it" (26). Before her life ends she does see her family once more, but the novelist has created an irrational chasm between town and country, and in the process she implies that Africans are intolerant and vengeful.

We are supposed to feel good about Pauline because she lives long enough (just barely) to see the blossoming friendship of Walter and Michelle. (Also Walter becomes a successful movie star.) But the assumptions about Pauline being "in her place" are never challenged, and the union of Walter and Michelle is as offstage as the writer can make it without altogether removing them from this planet. The writer uses a few terse lines to tell us that Michelle is in the hill country with Walter's family:

> Elangeni.
>   The hills.
>   The love of the brave and the young.
>   The birth of an infant, a young brave child,
>   crying out its message of wisdom to the waiting
>   world of eagles-flying-high, and seagulls and
>   bees and butterflies, a child that would be a man.
>   Michelle saw all these and was complete. Her river flowed [91].

The "message of wisdom" is contrasted in the novel to messages of race prejudice, messages which are blatant and carry the author's unmistakable disapproval. For example, when Michelle is visited by her friend Tanya, the insensitive visitor asks: "Why did you hang around with that Walter? He's black, you know, and we aren't supposed to hang around with them. ... Your Dad says he caused your accident. Did he push you into the road?" (22). Also Rupert, Michelle's cousin, is a proselytizing racist: "[Walter's] black, isn't he? ... Isn't that strange? ... It's just not ... normal.... I've been out with girls, but I wouldn't take a black girl out for anything" (49-50). To oppose these young fascists is no problem, but they are juxtaposed with Walter's peer group, and all the reader learns about them is that they are tsotsis, thugs who stab Walter in the face with a knife.

Walter's many-dimensioned anguish will supposedly compel readers to accept this stage-managed love affair. If, however, we are to understand that a romance existed between these young people, how do we estimate their ability to weather the storm of family and friends, all the interferring outsiders who are not prepared to give the couple a chance? Professor Totemeyer's hopeful analysis—that "African mythology is increasingly being fused with western ... values" while "the move towards a common southern African culture identity is gaining momentum through juvenile literature"—is not a convincing argument at this time. It will not become a reality until a balance is established in the educational system. A work of fiction needs to be culturally informed because the ways of a people are not trifles to those who share a communal heritage.

Images produced by Western writers for children are not currently representational. Symbols generally denigrate the African personality and lend support to Anglo-Saxon dreams of superiority. Character-types do not acknowledge black consciousness nor the centuries-long efforts of blacks. In *Streams to Rivers*, the cultural ideals of the blacks are either downgraded or trivialized. And finally, the protagonists become caricatures in the hands of the novelist as she strives to make what is unbelievable look and feel real.

Conclusion

Anticipating a cultural "new dawn" can be a constructive exercise, but cultural mutuality is its only conceivable foundation. Thus one wonders about the over-exuberant praise bestowed on the Smith and Harries novels. Additionally, Professor Totemeyer's accolades appeared in *Bookbird*, the official publication of the International Board on Books for Young People (IBBY). This organization and its editorial decisions carry weight because institutions concerned with children's books and cultural exchange are rare. It is vital that the white supremacy myth be denied any validation in an arena that we label "international."

If the world community encourages equality, then an optimistic viewpoint will gain some credibility. Then the world's children will indeed be served.

Works Cited

Achebe, Chinua. *Hopes and Impediments: Selected Essays.* New York: Doubleday, 1989.
Biko, Steve. *I Write What I Like.* (A selection of his writings ed. by Aelred Stubbs C.R.) London: Heinemann, 1987. (Originally published in 1978).
Harries, Ann. *The Sound of the Gora.* London: Heinemann, 1980.
Hirson, Baruch. *Year of Fire, Year of Ash: The Soweto Revolt: Roots of a Revolution?* London: Zed Press, 1979.
Smith, Janet. *Streams to Rivers.* Cape Town, S.A.: Maskew Miller Longman, 1988.
Totemeyer, Andree-Jeanne. "Impact of African Mythology on South African Juvenile Literature (Part 2)." *Bookbird* 30:3 (Sept., 1992): 10-15.

Through African Eyes

An Interview with Yulisa Amadu Maddy
*About Recent Picture Books**

Yulisa Amadu Maddy is a Sierra Leonean playwright, theater director, performing artist, choreographer, and novelist. In addition to his teaching and creative work in Sierra Leone, Zambia, and Nigeria, he has worked for the B.B.C., London, and Radio Denmark. He is founder and director of Gbakanda Afrikan Tiata which won the Edinburgh Festival Fringe First Award for its production of "Pulse" in 1979. Maddy was senior Fulbright scholar at the University of Maryland, Baltimore County, and Morgan State University 1985–86 and has been a visiting professor in several American universities. His publications include *Obasai and Other Plays* (1961) and the novel *No Past, No Present, No Future* (1973). During a recent professorship at the University of Iowa, he read numerous picture books about Africa and became interested in the images and messages they project. We questioned him about the books published during and after 1988.

WLB: As librarians and book critics working with the young, we want to encourage the publishing of good books about Africa and make wise judgments about those currently in print. Can you establish for us a frame of reference about Africa?

YAM: Perhaps we need to establish a frame of reference about Africa, perhaps not. My premise here is that the West (Euro-Americans) must stop treating Africa as if it is in or belongs to another planet. The continent of Africa, like any of the other five continents, has as great a physical and cultural variety. Africa is a continent of nations and not (just) warring

Wilson Library Bulletin, June 1995. Reprinted by permission, H.W. Wilson. This interview, which was conducted by Donnarae MacCann and Olga Richard, is presented here in a slightly expanded form.

tribes and clansmen as portrayed by the Western media. For well over five hundred years, Africa has remained a disturbing phenomenon to the Western mind. It is not surprising that Westerners created barbaric images about Africa and Africans; images that go back about five hundred years are still there, refusing to go away. Out of these false and distorted images have evolved stereotypes that have been preserved and institutionalized. The very people who created these stereotypic images and who have continued to perpetuate them are the people and institutions that have made Africa what it is today. It is therefore not surprising that most people who are writing and illustrating picture books about Africa go to those institutions where they get fabricated/false information.

WLB: Will you help us gain a clearer perception of some specific misrepresentations, especially the often-repeated representation of Africa as "backward"?

YAM: Misrepresentations come in different modes; they are present in different evaluation processes, assume a variety of colorations; they are sometimes used as an ally to justify value judgments.

It can be very dangerous when fantasy is mistaken for reality. Through the media, Africa has been misrepresented to the young, the old, the literate and illiterate. In some of the books that I have been reading, I find typical examples of the ongoing misrepresentations by writers and illustrators. For example, *The Market Lady and the Mango Tree* by Pete and Mary Watson (Tambourine, 1994) is the old Western-oriented story that Africans will simply squander any money they get on European objects. False assumptions, like embellishments, are embedded in the tale vis-à-vis African aspirations, business malpractices, and relations with children and community. When the nameless "market lady" hordes the fruits of a community-owned mango tree, she is presented as the grabbing individual. She is stereotypically vain and chaotic, misusing her car (a Mercedes Benz, the neocolonial symbol of power and status in Africa). She is part of a larger misrepresentation of the African society; that is, the children who gather around wanting the mangos but have no money to pay, and the community in which she operates do not respond to her corrupt malpractices in ways that express African values. The presentation of events and situations is one-sided. Neither the children nor the other market traders are seen as able to thwart the woman's graft and greed. No one in his/her right mind, no matter how greedy, would claim a mango tree in the market place as his/her property. Even a madman who by some coincidence might decide to squat under that tree would have to share the mangos with the children, or he would be forced to leave.

In *Charlie's House*, by Reviva Schermbrucker and illustrated by Niki Daly (Viking, 1991), a boy witnesses his mother's confrontation with a builder whose workmanship is bad. The attitude of the builder is that of "I know what is good for you." However, the message here focuses on low aspirations centered on the so-called "backwardness" of a boy who revels in the creations he can make from mud. The boy's inspiration was in response to a society that has failed to respond to the needs of the people.

Does an African child's imagination center around the glories of mud? Is it true that Africans are content to live in squalor and play in open sewers? Are African children to assume they will forever be deprived of a decent life and must single-handedly make up the difference with handouts from garbage?

Galimoto by Karen Lynn Williams, illustrated by Catherine Stock (Lothrop, Lee, and Shepard, 1990) also refers to people apparently too backward to recognize talent or even support a boy's ingenuity as a wire sculptor. He is in a largely antagonistic relationship with his community as he searches for discarded wires. The reader is given no hint as to what lies behind the frustration of the people or the cause for the hostility toward the child. Instead the author turns the child into a wire thief, since his people are too "primitive" to recognize a child's skills or even offer to a child a normal atmosphere of nurturing.

The image of "backwardness" carries with it innuendoes that are hidden in some of these texts in very subtle ways. Western missionaries, in their earliest contacts with Africa, ventured into the interior of Africa, thereby coming sometimes face to face with African traditions and customary practices which they could not fathom or understand. They then found it useful to speak of the "savage heathen," and the less adventurous colonial administrators emphasized the same theme, adding the "dark continent" myth.

It is therefore not surprising that today Peace Corps representatives, international project workers, and exchange students bring the same message into books for the young (even when they borrow from authentic African myths and legends) as can be seen in some of the books we are discussing.

WLB: Two books by Western families on assignment in Africa are odd mixtures of childhood perspectives and the slanted views of their parents. Will you talk about this ambivalence?

YAM: You are referring to *When Africa Was Home* by Karen Lynn Williams, illustrated by Floyd Cooper (Orchard, 1991), and *Learning to Swim in Swaziland* by Nila K. Leigh (Scholastic, 1993). *Learning to Swim in Swaziland*, we are informed, is a child's-eye view of a South African country. That the story was written by a child makes it all the more interesting. In both books we are sharing the relationships and experiences of children, or so it seems, until you realize that in the background the child is not "free" to enjoy the freedom of innocent interrelationships and the joy of being at one with and at home in a different environment.

The child in *Learning to Swim* is adapting to her new locale, participating in local customs and generally expressing the innocence of childhood that can be expected of the young before institutionalized indoctrination sets in. Children, in my opinion, do not know anything about color in terms of race and prejudice until they are instructed in that mindset, until they can be made to explain things in ways that parrot an adult voice.

For example, in this book *Learning to Swim*, the young narrator is the author of the book. She dwells upon symbols of deprivation (no toy stores, no television, no school bus, no paved roads, no adequate supply of pencils, no electricity, and so on). There is no doubt that there is an adult bias behind the false information about the African children lacking jewelry and using pieces of straw in their ears in place of earrings. Actually, the straw is just a means of keeping open the hole when ears are initially pierced. Intermittently in this text, the missionary attitude of Africa as inferior is laid over the child's impression that Africa (not Africans) is unique and worth knowing.

Similarly, in *When Africa Was Home* the child protagonist is at home in the new locale, but the author is not. The integration into African traditional ways of life is incomprehensible for the author to imagine. She is struck by the "fear of the unknown," yet for some unexplained reason, the white child is allowed to visit freely in the African family house and become a "member" of that family. On the other end of the relationship, the African child with whom the white child spends his time and learns from while growing up is never invited into the Euro-American house. Peter, the white American boy, sees his African friend and her parents as "family," whereas Peter's family sees only a "nannie" who is a paid servant to be used while they are on assignment overseas.

Mutuality, a basic human element, is the missing ingredient here. Peter's temporary (genuine and innocent) openness to new friendships will soon lapse into a "them" and "us" neo-colonial perspective, because the reader of this book is given this subliminal message from the outset. To the white adults, Africa is the same "wilderness" projected in Western popular culture. It could not be a "home" unless under white subordination.

WLB: In a review of Virginia Kroll's *African Brothers and Sisters* in the *New York Times Book Review* (Sept. 5, 1993), the West African scholar Kwame Anthony Appiah criticizes the numerous errors of fact and inference in that children's book (even the map is incorrectly drawn). Do you find this a recurring problem in your book sample?

YAM: This issue of inauthenticity occurs in different ways. Sometimes it mars an otherwise commendable work, as in Ann Grifalconi's *Flyaway Girl* (Little, Brown, 1992). Generally this narrative captures the African spirit in a pleasing poetic style, but the mistakes in the text confuse Western and Eastern Africa. The Masai of East Africa cannot be associated with the Benin mask that is shown in the illustrations (a mask that is well-known to art historians and anthropologists) nor is the food (foufou) that is mentioned an East African food. These are not trivial matters to the people of these different traditions. Sometimes misinformation is a politically important message, a distortion of history that serves to cover up the colonialist incursions. For example, Paul Geraughty's *The Hunter* (Brown, 1994) features a lost African child who must hide from dangerous African poachers who are decimating the elephant herds for their ivory. This is turning history on its head! The obsession with ivory (and its disastrous environmental consequences) is essentially European. And at a psychological level, this story repeats the notion of social chaos since the little girl's grandfather is the irresponsible adult who neglects the child and places her in mortal danger.

One Round Moon and a Star for Me by Ingrid Mennen, illustrated by Niki Daly (Orchard, 1994), and Grifalconi's *Osa's Pride* (Little, Brown 1990) indicate cultural inauthenticity in their Western style plotlines. African characters act so as to produce dramatic tensions which are essentially alien to the African spirit.

One Round Moon and a Star for Me is about a generation gap that might suggest itself to a Western writer, but the tale is not in an African mold. When the protagonist's brother is born, he asks his father, "Are you my father?" Where does such an idea come from? Unless this father has been an abusive parent, the love of the father for the son would never be called into question. And the child in Africa needs no reassurance in this regard. A question about being loved does not have to be asked, since the African child is happy with his/her family unless made to feel unhappy, and the context of the question in the story provides no clue of alienation. The boy at that age has no reason to wonder what misdeed he has been guilty of that he is not loved. Such trumped up dramatic effects misrepresent the culture world of the African family.

In *Osa's Pride* a young girl is proud to the point of conceit, and this unexplained sense of superiority separates her from the group. Again this seems like an idea imposed by a Western mind, since communal living does not typically generate behaviors that are so disruptive of group interrelationships. But assuming that Osa is inexplicably conceited, she would not turn red when reprimanded by her elders for this antisocial manner. Europeans blush, but Africans express such moods differently.

WLB: The "global village" idea (a concept embracing cultural and social equality) is a new direction in publishing. Will you comment on works that represent this tendency, e.g., *It Takes a Village* by Jane Cowen-Fletcher (Scholastic, Inc., 1994); *Lala Salama: An African Lullaby* by Hannah Heritage Bozylinsky (Philomel Books, 1993), *Bitter Bananas* by Isaac Olaleye and illustrated by Ed Young (Boyds Mills Press, 1994), *The Distant Talking Drum* by Isaac Olaleye and illustrated by Frane Lessac (Wordsong, Boyds Mills Press, 1995); *The Ancestor Tree* by T. Obinkaram Echewa and illustrated by Christy Hale (Lodestar Books, Dutton, 1994); and *Big Boy* by Tololwa M. Mollel and illustrated by E. B. Lewis (Clarion Books, 1995)?

YAM: I want to believe that the "global village" is a reality, an indisputable reality just as is the European common market. However, such coalitions exist outside of the Africa I know and grew up in. As to real equality between the races, I have very serious doubts that it will ever come to fruition. If ever there is that chance, it will not be without confrontations: confrontation with bigotry, with materialism and neocolonialism. Equality means big "problems," and big problems are law problems, and law problems are expensive problems, and expensive problems can become threatening explosives.

Describing African village life can be interesting, entertaining, and instructive. *It Takes a Village* is a heart-warming story, confirming that in almost all African countries, people believe it when they say: it takes one person (parent) to give birth to a child; but the upbringing of every child born in the community is the responsibility of that community.

Euro-American author Cowen-Fletcher presents an African village community quite different and distinct from the usual chaotic, caricatured "limbo" where there are always wars between greedy and corrupt warlords. In the normalcy of everyday life, a little girl offers to help her mother care for her toddler brother, so that mom can concentrate on selling her wares in the marketplace. Before her wish is granted, the mother asks whether she understands this responsibility.

But at the crowded marketplace, the toddler wanders off, leaving sister in a state of panic. While the girl searches, the toddler, in his adventure, discovers the food seller who feeds him, the refreshment seller who gives him a cool drink, an old lady who so admires him that she gives him a bath, and so on. The message of this story is: village life is "caring and sharing," but it takes a sensitive and unprejudiced Euro-American writer to understand the proverb, "It takes a village to raise a child."

The Ancestor's Tree is the story of an old man, Nna Nna Anya Mele, who has no children of his own but is loved and respected by the village children. He tells them stories and teaches them songs and parables about the "old once upon a time" before they were born. Now the old man knows he has but a very short time left to live and there will be no one to plant for him on his grave an Ancestor Tree that, according to the tradition, should be planted in his memory. Not having an Ancestor Tree was symbolic of an incomplete and unfulfilled life. In most African traditions, it is believed that restless wandering spirits are ancestors whose missions were incomplete when they passed away. So before the old man died, the children adopted him as their parent, and after his burial, they convinced the authorities about the need for change and they finally had their request granted. Echewa's story is very delightful and revealing in many instances. First, the children made a promise and kept it. Second, the elders had ears to listen and understood the need for change without compromising any of the traditions of their people.

Bitter Bananas is a story that demonstrates for the reader how a united family and a unified community can protect itself and its property from any inside and/or outside force.

Apes are not the best of animals to be found in and around a village,

but they are sometimes present. Ironically, this story has a symbolic trickster twist to it. The invading "takers" (baboons) are no less human than
those whose motives and intentions are evil. As tricksters they consider
themselves indomitable until they are outwitted. But the story implies
that no matter how long, nothing lasts forever.

The Distant Talking Drum is educative and will enable the reader
to gain an accurate impression of the culture of the Yorubas. In this
group of poems, we encounter the African pride in the complete family
that is actively productive and responsible. In contrast to many books,
the father's influence, which is so vital to family life, is not obscured or
left out. Moreover, the writer does not suggest that outside influences
and directives are required to insure the life of the village. The happiness
of the community is dependent upon the traditional communal responsibility.

Big Boy includes the dream of every young boy. At his age his aspi-
ration to do great things and achieve the utmost is not unique, and he
longs for the independence that he sees allotted to his older brother. There
are children all over the world who, even though they come from deprived
homes, have ambitions which they nourish. They are sometimes encouraged by parents who know a cruel world awaits the child, especially in a
third-world country. But Mollel writes with optimism, and this story is
very appealing.

For the very youngest child, Wendy Hartmann's wildlife counting
book, *One Sun Rises* (illustrated by Nicolass Maritz, Dutton, 1994), and
Ifeoma Onyefulu's *"A" Is for Africa* (Cobblehill Books, 1993) complement
each other in a unique fashion. The wildlife counting book introduces
new and rare animals to the reader just as in *"A" Is for Africa* the writer
takes her readers to her village, introducing them to symbols, places, and
objects that they are not familiar with in the West. Hannah Heritage
Bozylinsky's *Lala Salama: An African Lullaby* (Philomel, 1993) mesmer-
izes with its "peace, sleep well" refrain and introduces the cattle-loving
Masai people.

WLB: One potentially authentic contact with Africa is through folktales,
but we have found in the retellings from other regions that material in a
preface or afterword is sometimes biased and historically invalid. If you
have found similar flaws, will you point them out to us? Will you show
where comparisons drawn with European folklore are made inappropri-
ately?

YAM: The African tale *The Iroko-Man*, by Phillis Gershator (illustrated by Holly C. Kim, Orchard Books, 1994), includes in its cover information that this tale is similar to the Brothers Grimm tale "Rumplestiltskin." There is nothing wrong with making comparisons, especially when the purpose is to educate as well as entertain. My objection is when the originality of the work is given to the wrong source. Worse still is when the theme of the stories is completely different and the motives and messages (from an African perspective) are incomparable. For example, Rumplestiltskin's greed is the central motivating factor. In contrast, need and desperation are primary to the villagers in *The Iroko-Man*, not just to the women. The Iroko-Man (a tree spirit) was part of their everyday life and was not an evil force. He would not have accepted the wooden effigy which was given in place of the real child promised him at the time of desperation. In Rumplestiltskin, the little man was alien to the culture of the miner's daughter. The greed of her father and the king brought the little man into her life. Her effort to keep her baby was natural, but that could not be said to mean that both stories are similar.

The issue of modern urban culture as a source of generating new tales as well as modernizing old ones has become the subject of many folklore studies all over the world. In the 1960s and '70s, dance ensembles from Africa toured the Western world performing traditional dances based on folktales that were dealing with historical and contemporary themes.

We cannot deny the authenticity of the African-Western contact; however, this contact can be likened to an East African anecdote that goes like this: "Once upon a time there was a hyena that said, 'Good morning' to the rock; the rock did not reply. 'Good morning, rock!' the hyena repeated, but still there was no answer. Then the hyena told the rock: 'Even if you don't answer me, you have heard my words'." Africa has been on the giving end, and the reality of it is that there are many picture-book folktales whose writers spend at most three years in one village and become African folklore "experts," turning for references and source materials to eighteenth-, nineteenth-, and early twentieth-century colonial sources. They seek out missionary, trader, settler, and anthropologist research notes and reports which are crammed with prejudices, distortions and misrepresentations of Africa. The worldview is the Western view and has nothing to do with Africa and Africans because we did not create it.

For example, Aardema's anthology, *Misoso* (Random House, 1996), is very informative in content but also misleading in its reliance on colonialist sources. In this collection, "The Toad's Trick" is a Kanuri (Nigerian) tale about the toad and the rat. The toad proposes to the rat a challenge. "I can do something you can't do." He (toad) can hop into the midst of a group of men and get away unhurt and the rat can't. This he does. Rat, on the other hand, in accepting the challenge, nearly gets killed. This is a universal and recognizable reality; we know that a lot of people have lost their lives foolishly trying to prove what they are not. But in the "afterword" of this story, Ms. Aardema introduces her readers to the Rev. S.W. Koelle, who in 1854 had written a textbook of folklore, the second book of African folklore ever published in English. The unfortunate and sad part of the "afterword" is this explanation: "As in this tale, it is typical in Kanuri culture that during the daytime the men would sit under trees while the women worked in their huts or gardens." A "wise saying" from the time of Koelle's book allegedly reveals the tribe's attitude towards women: "Who are more in number, men or women?" The answer: "women, because men who listen to what women say are counted as women." This text, we are told, was used in mission schools in what is now Zambia. One can deduce from such a story that the Rev. Koelle lived in the country of the Kanuri people, but he never understood their culture and did not respect their lifestyle.

In "The Boogy Man's Wife," a Mano tale about an independent woman, Ms. Aardema makes the mistake in her "afterword" of telling us that Liberia was founded by freed American slaves who returned to Africa. I think we must begin here to correct this outrageous falsity. Africa was not discovered. It was there. These freed slaves met the Mano people and were welcome to stay and set up their mission.

Geographically and historically, Ms. Aardema meets some challenges; however, she should allow interested readers to do their own research, rather than impose on them a distorted Western worldview.

WLB: Several African authors have entered the picture book field recently, and some non–Africans have written credible tales in the folk traditions. Will you describe some of your favorites?

YAM: I enjoyed reading M. Mollel's *The Orphan Boy* (illustrated by Paul Morin, Clarion Books, 1990), *A Promise to the Sun* (illustrated by Beatriz Vidal, Little, Brown, 1992), and *The King and the Tortoise* (illustrated by Kathy Blankley, Clarion Books, 1993). These folktales have a lot in common with those adapted by Euro-American writers, except that this

African writer does not refer to, nor depend on, the confirmation of references that are obsolete. If *The King and the Tortoise* had been written by a Westerner, I suspect that the foreword/afterword would have referred the readers to Hans Christian Andersen's "The Emperor's New Clothes." Similarly, *The Orphan Boy* by Mollel exposes us to a miracle story that has counterparts around the world, while Deborah M. Newton Chocolate's *Imani in the Belly* (illustrated by Alex Boles, Bridgewater Books, 1994) is a story that could easily be referenced to a Biblical story (the Jonah tale), except for the fact that the beast has swallowed more than one. This is a political story of liberation and it follows the traditional pattern where the ancestor spirit of Imani (her deceased mother) appears to her in a dream and instructs her [on] what to do to save her children. In following the instructions, she saves cattle and villagers as well as her children.

The Perfect Orange, a Tale from Ethiopia, retold by Frank P. Araujo (Rayve, 1994), and *Nobiah's Well*, a modern African tale by Donna W. Guthrie (Ideal Children's Books, 1993), introduce the reader to that very special outgoing kindliness of the African spirit: the spirit of giving. In *Nobiah's Well* (illustrated by Rob Roth), the hero's mother was angry and demanded of her son: "Why would you waste precious water on animals?" Logically, the little boy retorted: "They feel the same thirst as we do." Such an answer could well be utilized in our present-day reality. Correspondingly, we witness, but on a very different level, this theme in *The Perfect Orange* (illustrated by Xiao Jun Li). Tshai, the orphan girl, is rewarded by Negus (the Ethiopian ruler) and Ato Jib, the Lord Hyena, is humiliated by the Negus after his greedy motives are exposed.

In retrospect, I ask myself why is it so impossible for people of different races to live and respect and love their differences. This issue of insider/outsider status is suggested in two tales. In *King of Another Country*, by Fiona French (Scholastic, 1993), the protagonist, named Ojo, was not like the other people in the village. He refuses to help anyone and refuses to say "yes" to any request. One day on his way out of the village, he keeps saying "No, no, no!" In the forest he picks a juicy fruit and a fierce creature springs out and tells him he should "ask his permission first." "No," said Ojo. In time Ojo becomes reconciled to learning when to say "yes" and when to say "no." My interpretation to this story could be one of many; i.e., it could refer to political indoctrination where the converted/indoctrinated ones reject what they are until they discover for themselves who they really are. On another level, Ojo is just a character in a story who shows us that some people have no mind of their own and therefore cannot make individual decisions.

Sunguru and Leopard, by Barbara Knutson (Little, Brown, 1933), best illustrates the possibility of accommodating people for what and who they are and not because they are different, foreign and alien. Why and how could Sunguru, the hare, being the smaller animal, outwit the leopard and drive him out of a house they have both built, each in his own time and without knowing the other is a neighbor? A beautiful minority/majority situational question.

WLB: Works of history are typically presented in a nonpictorial format and geared for older readers, but *Shaka, King of the Zulus*, by Diane Stanley and Peter Vennema (illustrated by Diane Stanley, Morrow, 1988), is an exception. Since this title was selected for inclusion in the *New York Times* "Best Illustrated Book" list for 1988, it is likely to have a wider circulation than most books. What is your assessment of how Shaka and his nation are portrayed?

YAM: First, let me say that I am not a historian. Having said that, I want to say that there are many great African historical figures but very few have been made into a legend as has Emperor Shaka. Shaka has been compared with Napoleon, Julius Caesar, and Alexander the Great as a military genius. But he was more than that. As an introduction, the Stanley/Vennema biography could have helped the Euro-American public get to know about the Zulus and how Shaka transformed that society and the thinking of the whole of Central and Southern Africa. The life and times of Shaka from conception to assassination is one giant epic. There are, however, quite a number of errors in this book which could mislead the reader and confirm the notions of white traders and others—those colonizers who depicted Shaka as a "master-killer" and a "ruthless ruler." For instance, the writers stated that "throughout Shaka's life he ruled through force and fear—that is how he made his soldiers obey him, and that is how his army won battles."

There is no military conquest without military discipline, and when Shaka assumed full authority of the Zulu state, he made it clear that they had to have changes if they were to survive as a free nation. The Zulus at the advent of Shaka's leadership were a small nation that had neither the will to fight wars nor the ability to do so. Shaka, it is said, "reorganized the society and created the military machinery starting from the beginning." Unlike Napoleon and Alexander, who found already existing armies, Shaka built his own army of disciplined warriors and established a political ethic that brought together a disparate and powerful clan.

Moreover, the history and greatness of Shaka, the legendary Zulu hero, is incomplete without including the mother and the important role his mother played. The African mother is not a "shadow." Her role as we know it in African society is that of a teacher and it is said that "the greatest rulers" are those who had "the greatest mothers" who taught them. We learn very little in the Stanley/Vennema biography about Nandi, Shaka's mother, and the very important part she played as a social and political teacher in his early life. Nor do we hear about her influence as a strategist and as one responsible for developing the "raison d'etre" for the expansion of the political boundaries of the Zulu state. Also the encounter and relationship between Shaka and the whites, especially the British, has been scantily glossed over so that the reader does not get to know that Shaka kept a court well established in the art of foreign diplomacy and that he had a British general named King to whom he gave the coastal region to administer.

Looking at the sources from which the writers got their information, it seems that they did not take cognizance of another major root source—the African historical and oral sources. Some of the commentaries on Shaka are unfortunate because they are based on secondary white sources—sources whose colonial strategy was not only to conquer but also "to dismantle heroic images and heroic personages of the African people" and replace them with their own.

The illustrations in this book look impressive at first glance. Taking a much closer look, I could not discern whether the women were wearing a modern knee length skirt or whether it was skin very neatly pleated. Shaka had his hair plaited while he waited for a new spear at the blacksmiths. These misleading images mar a book which could have helped to bridge the historical gap and pave the way for the introduction of other great African rulers like Osei Ttu of Asante, Obaseki of Benin, Lobengula of Zimbabwe and many others with whom the West came into contact and some of whose help contributed greatly to the rise and wealth of Western civilization as we know it today.

WLB: Should critics, publishers, and librarians be particularly alert to subtle visual messages, since the media still make use of biased images with pretwentieth-century origins?

YAM: In dealing with picture books, we are dealing with words and illustrations. Both types of textual content, including paintings and photographs, need to be interpreted carefully and critically as documents. It could be a serious mistake to take a photograph or a painting for granted as being "true," more true than words, which can lie. Photographs and paintings can distort; sometimes we find in them elements of indelible propaganda. To be alert is imperative since we are dealing with African materials in the hands of mainly white writers, illustrators and photographers, white editors, publishers, and critics.

In concluding, let me return to your initial question about "frame of reference." Our African ancestors endured slavery's dehumanization and survived. Christian missionaries, traders, and settlers of colonial origin ravaged the continent of Africa, plundered the wealth and human resources, but still they survived. Today, the legacies of neocolonial, independent African states are poverty, disease, malnutrition, drought, civil war, brain-drain, corruption, and the industrial world "rape-off" in token-aid support. Still, Africa stands "sternly beautiful in its loveliness" in spite of its depth of gloom and terror. Its richness of color, its silver of endless sand, its lakes and swamps and jungles—all are there as frames of reference for those who want to unravel the phenomenon—the so-called "Dark Continent."

They say that "truth" can be relative; what I ask is, if you feel the concern to find out about the African ethos, take a bold step and cross over the borderline to my side. You don't have to join me. Just cross over and see how things really are from the continent of the "old and ever new and incredibly ancient Africa," from the African people's point of view without an "ism," bias, or prejudice. Writers, critics, and whoever takes up the challenge and crosses over the borderline could find themselves in direct confrontation with much more than they had bargained for. But why not? Who says the "truth" is easy to digest when there could be so much to lose?

Epilogue

Several discoveries that are broad in scope resulted from our examination of the novels and critical reviews featured in this book. The way cultural imperialism still flourishes in the 1990s in the world of children's books was surprising. The vitality and pervasiveness of this destructive phenomenon was unexpected, as was the blatant manner in which the white supremacy myth is expressed. It seems as if the use of Africa as a venue for contemporary racism is broadly accepted.

Another "finding" is the degree to which neocolonialist thought is identical in the United States, Great Britain, and South Africa. In creating portraits of blacks, authors who write for children and young adults approach their task with similarly biased assumptions. The indigenous African population is described as simultaneously violence-prone and lacking any initiative for self-expression, self-determination, and even self-defense. Both the beastly and the childish characterizations (throwbacks to nineteenth-century stereotyping) are heavily utilized by current writers in all three nations. Given the histories and economic structures of these regions—given the long-term dependence on forced labor and peonage—the overlapping forms of cultural oppression should not have surprised us. And in fact our "surprises" were slightly differentiated: that racism is still so *overt* in the children's literature field puzzled one of us (Donnarae); that children's novelists have staked out Africa as the site of so much neocolonialist *activity* was a new discovery for a Sierra Leonian playwright (Amadu).

These realizations have underscored the necessity of taking sides. The Latino writer, Pablo Neruda, has stated in "Toward the Splendid City" that his attitude as an artist must include solidarity with the masses. He explains:

> ... if my attitude gave and still gives rise to bitter ... objections, the truth is that I can find no other way for a writer ... if we want the darkness to

blossom, if we are concerned that the millions of people who have learned neither to read us nor to read at all, who still cannot write or write to us, are to feel at home in the dignity without which it is impossible for them to be complete human beings.

For I believe that my duties as a poet involve friendship not only with the rose and with symmetry, ... but also with unrelenting human occupations [quoted in San Juan, xv–xvi].

Artistic achievement and social value are not placed in opposition by this author. Nor are they treated as mutually exclusive by the Nigerian novelist and critic, Chinua Achebe. "Art," he says, "is important, but so is education of the kind I have in mind." He continues:

I would be quite satisfied if my novels ... did no more than teach my readers that their past—with all its imperfections—was not one long night of savagery from which the first Europeans acting on God's behalf delivered them [quoted in San Juan, 137].

While a neocolonialist message permeates Western novels for young people, the literary artists in colonized regions stress social responsibility and the unbreakable links between citizenship and other aspects of living. To quote Amado V. Hernandez, a Filipino writer: "The days are over when the artist was a new Narcissus who, before the mirror of the stream, marvelled and adored the shadow of his own self." Hernandez adds that "The artist is now a witness and part of the immediate present. ... He [she] contributes to the whole [of society] but also receives from the whole" (quoted in San Juan, 136).

An essential thread running through these statements is the idea that artists must be true to the particulars of the subject they lay before their readers. They will probably not make truthful inferences and plausible allusions if they have assimilated a historically alien worldview or have become absorbed solely in "the shadow of his [her] own self." The failures in the novels we have discussed bear out this thesis. But this approach to multiculturalism is not accepted in all children's book circles. Marc Aronson, writing in *The Horn Book* for March/April, 1995, states that "the multiculturalism that parades 'authenticity' and pretends that *a* culture has *a* view ... is now something of a shibboleth. ... But that view of cultural diversity is also wrong" (163–64). His concern, he says, relates to "a real problem for reviewers"—namely, that they will be asked to "make exceptions for obviously weak books that are ethnically pure." This is a false dichotomy. The essential unity between form and substance is stated simply by Feng Hsueh-feng:

... social value, understood not in a narrow but in a broad sense, must be realized through artistry in literature [through art's method, mechanism and power]. [However] if a work of art does not produce social value, then what "artistic value" will it attain? [quoted in Nazareth, xxiv].

In Africa, as in other parts of the colonized and neocolonized world, the interplay between form and substance in an artistic work is subtle, fluid, and amenable to no pat formula. A society and its artists are concerned "with every aspect of its affairs, private and public, transient and enduring, past, present and future" (Chinweizu, 253). But this is not to say that cultural imperialism is tolerable. It is intolerable. Dennis Brutus' "Voices of Challenge" says it best:

> From the dust
> from the mud
> from the fields
> the voices will rise
> the voices of challenge.
>
> Do not be mistaken,
> make no mistake,
> you will think they are asleep.
> You will be wrong—
> they will arise—
> the voices will rise—
> the voices of challenge
> will challenge you.
>
> The bones of those who died in the bush,
> the blood spilt in the dust of Soweto,
> of Sebokeng, of Sharpeville,
> of Bishu, of Boipatong, of Kwa Mashu
> will challenge you,
> of Langa, Nyanga and KwazaKele
> will challenge you.
>
> When there are compromises
> they will challenge you
> Where there are betrayals
> they will challenge you.
>
> Do not rest easy, do not be deceived
> those who have suffered and died
> those who have sacrificed for freedom
> their voices will challenge you
>
> Endlessly, until we are free [18].

Works Cited

Achebe, Chinua. *Hopes and Impediments: Selected Essays*. New York: Doubleday, 1989.

Aronson, Mark. "A Mess of Stories." *Horn Book* 71:2 (March/April, 1995): 163–68.

Brutus, Dennis. *Still the Sirens*. Tesuque, N.M.: Penny Whistle Press, 1993.

Chinweizu, Onwuchekwa Jemie, and Ihechukwu Madubuike. *Toward the Decolonization of African Literature, Vol.I: African Fiction and Poetry and Their Critics*. Enugu, Nigeria: Fourth Dimension Publishers, 1980.

Nayareth, Peter. *The Third World Writer: His Social Responsibility*. Nairobi: Kenya Literature Bureau, 1978.

San Juan, E., Jr. *Ruptures, Schisms, Interventions: Cultural Revolution in the Third World*. Manila, Philippines: De La Salle University Press, 1988.

Selected Bibliography

Africa: Historical and Cultural Studies

Achebe, Chinua. *Hopes and Impediments: Selected Essays.* New York: Doubleday, 1989.

Arnold, Stephen. *African Literature Studies: The Present State/L' État Présent.* Washington: Three Continents Press, Inc., 1985.

Bascome, William. *African Art in Cultural Perspective—An Introduction.* New York: W. W. Norton, 1973.

Berman, Bruce. *Control & Crisis in Colonial Kenya: The Dialectic of Domination.* London: James Currey; Athens: Ohio University Press, 1990.

Biko, Steve. *I Write What I Like.* London: Heinemann Educational Books, Ltd., 1987. (Originally published in 1978).

Chinweizu, Onwuchekwa Jemie, and Ihechukwu Madubuike. *Toward the Decolonization of African Literature. Volume 1: African Fiction and Poetry and Their Critics.* Enugu, Nigeria: Fourth Dimension Publishers, 1980.

Davidson, Basil. *African Awakening.* London: Jonathan Cape, 1955.

_____. *Can Africa Survive? Arguments Against Growth Without Development.* Boston and Toronto: Little, Brown, 1974.

_____. *Modern Africa: Social and Political History.* 3d ed. London and New York: Longman, 1994.

_____. *The People's Cause, A History of Guerrillas in Africa.* London and New York: Longman, 1981.

_____. *The Search for Africa: A History in the Making.* London: James Currey, 1994.

Emenyonu, Ernest N. *Literature and Society: Selected Essays on African Literature.* Nigeria: Zim Pan African Publishers, 1986.

Fredrickson, George M. *Black Liberation: A Comparative History of Black Ideologies in the United States and South Africa.* New York and Oxford: Oxford University Press, 1995.

_____. *White Supremacy: A Comparative Study in American & South African History.* New York and Oxford: Oxford University Press, 1981.

Gillon Werner. *A Short History of African Art.* Penguin Books, 1984.

Hanlon, J. *Beggar Your Neighbours: Apartheid Power in South Africa.* Bloomington: Indiana University Press; London: James Currey Press, 1986.

Hirson, Baruch. *Year of Fire, Year of Ash; The Soweto Revolt: Roots of a Revolution?* London: Zed Press, 1979.

Kaba, Lansine. "Historical Consciousness and Politics in Africa." In *Black Studies:*

Theory, Method, and Cultural Perspectives. Ed. Talmadge Anderson. Pullman: Washington State University Press, 1990; pp. 43–51.

Kunene, Mazisi. *Emperor Shaka, the Great—A Zulu Epic.* London: Heinemann, 1979.

Lawson, William. *The Western Star: The Theme of the Been-to in West African Fiction.* Athens: Ohio University Press, 1982.

Mermeistein, David. *The Anti–Apartheid Reader: The Struggle Against White Racist Rule in South Africa.* New York: Grove Press, 1987.

Mutiso, Gideon Cyrus, M. *Socio-Political Thought in African Literature: Weusi?* New York: Barnes & Noble, 1974.

Nafziger, E. Wayne. *Inequality in Africa.* New York.: Cambridge University Press, 1988.

Ngugi, wa Thiong'o. *Decolonizing the Mind: The Politics of Language in African Literature.* Portsmouth, N.H.: Heinemann; London: James Currey, 1986.

_____. *Moving the Centre: The Struggle for Cultural Freedoms.* Portsmouth, N.H.: Heinemann; London: Currey, 1993.

Somerville, Keith. *Foreign Military Intervention in Africa.* London: Pinter Publishers, 1990.

Imperialism: Social and Literary Studies

Ashcroft, Bill, Gareth Griffiths, and Helen Tiffin. *The Empire Writes Back: Theory and Practice in Post-Colonial Literatures.* London and New York: Routledge, 1989.

Brantlinger, Patrick. "Victorians and Africans: The Genealogy of the Myth of the Dark Continent." *Critical Inquiry* 12:1 (Autumn, 1985): 166–203.

Césaire, Aimé. *Discourse on Colonialism.* New York and London: Monthly Review Press, 1972.

Cohen, William B. "Literature and Race: 19th Century French Fiction, Blacks and Africa, 1800–1880." *Race & Class,* 16:2 (Oct. 1974): 181–205.

February, V.A. *Mind Your Colour: The "Coloured" Stereotype in South African Literature.* London and Boston: Kegan Paul Pub., 1981.

Fryer, Peter. *Black People in the British Empire: An Introduction.* London: Pluto Press, 1988.

Godlewska, Anne, and Neil Smith, eds. *Geography and Empire.* Cambridge, Mass., and Oxford, England: Blackwell, 1994.

Hobson, John A. *Imperialism: A Study.* Ann Arbor: University of Michigan Press, 1965. (Originally published in 1902).

Katz, Wendy R. *Rider Haggard and the Fiction of Empire: A Critical Study of British Imperial Fiction.* New York: Cambridge University Press, 1987.

Killam, G.D. *Africa in English Fiction, 1874–1939.* Ibadan: University Press, 1968.

Mackenzie, John. *Imperialism & Popular Culture.* Manchester, England: Manchester University Press, 1986.

Mangan, J.A. *Benefits Bestowed? Education and British Imperialism.* Manchester, England, and New York: Manchester University Press, 1988.

Newsinger, John. "Lord Greystoke and Darkest Africa: The Politics of the Tarzan Stories." *Race & Class,* 28:2 (Autumn, 1986): 59–71.

Pieterse, Jan Nederveen. *White on Black: Images of Africa and Blacks in Western Popular Culture.* New Haven and London: Yale University Press, 1992.

Said, Edward. *Culture and Imperialism.* New York: Alfred A. Knopf, 1993.

San Juan, E., Jr. *Ruptures, Schisms, Interventions: Cultural Revolution in the Third World*. Manila, Philippines: De La Salle University Press, 1988.

Shohat, Ella, and Robert Stam. *Unthinking Eurocentrism: Multiculturalism and the Media*. London and New York: Routledge, 1994.

Street, Brian. *The Savage in Literature: Representations of "Primitive" Society in English Fiction, 1858–1920*. London: Routledge & Kegan Paul, 1975.

Tiffin, Chris, and Alan Lawson. *De-scribing Empire: Post-colonialism & Textuality*. London and New York: Routledge, 1994.

Imperialism, Africa, and Children's Literature

Davies, Godfrey. "G.A. Henty & History." *Huntington Library Quarterly* 18:2 (Feb. 1955): 159–67.

Dixon, Bob. *Catching Them Young 2: Political Ideas in Children's Fiction*. London: Pluto Press, 1977.

Dunae, Patrick. "Boys' Literature and the Idea of Empire, 1870–1914." *Victorian Studies* 24:1 (Autumn 1980): 105–21.

_____. "Boys' Literature and the Idea of Race: 1870–1900." *Wascana Review* 12:1 (Spring 1979).

"Education in South Africa: Five Personal Accounts." *Interracial Books for Children Bulletin* 16:5 & 6 (1985): 16–21.

Guy, Arnold. *Held Fast for England: G.A. Henty, Imperialist Boys' Writer*. London: Hamish Hamilton, 1980.

Hall, Susan J. "What Do Textbooks Teach Our Children About Africa?" *Interracial Books for Children Bulletin* 9:3 (1978): 3–10.

Hannabuss, Stuart. "Ballantyne's Message of Empire." In *Imperialism and Juvenile Literature*. Ed. Jeffrey Richards. Manchester, England, and New York: Manchester University Press, 1989; pp. 53–71.

Hedge, Ann, and Anne Marie Davies. "Images of Africa in British History Texts." *Interracial Books for Children Bulletin* 10:4 (1979).

Huttenback, Robert A. "G.A. Henty and the Imperial Stereotype." *Huntington Library Quarterly* 29:1 (November 1965).

_____. "G.A. Henty and the Vision of Empire." *Encounter* 35 (July 1979): 46–53.

Khorana, Meena. *Africa in Literature for Children and Young Adults: An Annotated Bibliography of English-Language Books*. Westport, Conn., and London: Greenwood Press, 1994.

_____. "Apartheid in South African Children's Fiction." *Children's Literature Association Quarterly* 13:2 (1988): 52–56.

Kohl, Herbert. *Should We Burn Babar? Essays on Children's Literature and the Power of Stories*. New York: New Press, 1995.

Kuya, Dorothy. "In British Schoolbooks, It's Still Yesterday." *Interracial Books for Children Bulletin* 6:8 (1975): 2.

James, Louis. "Tom Brown's Imperialist Sons." *Victorian Studies* 17:1 (September 1973).

Journal of African Children's and Youth Literature (JACYL). Ed. Osayimwense Osa. Itta Bena, Mississippi: Dept. of English & Foreign Languages, Mississippi Valley State University.

Logan, Mawuena. *Africa Through Victorian Eyes: George Alfred Henty and the Fiction of Empire*. Ph.D. diss., University of Iowa, 1996.

_____. "Henty and the Ashantis." *Children's Literature Association Quarterly* 16:2 (Summer 1991): 82–86.

_____. "Pushing the Imperial/Colonial Agenda: G.A. Henty's *The Young Colonists*." *Journal of African Children's and Youth Literature* 6 (1994/95).

"Long Struggle for Change." (Brief biographies of South African liberationists). *Interracial Books for Children Bulletin* 16:5 & 6 (1985): 22–27.

MacCann, Donnarae. "Hugh Lofting." In *Writers for Children: Critical Studies of Major Authors Since the Seventeenth Century*. Ed. Jane M. Bingham New York: Scribner's, 1988.

Mangan, J.A. "Noble Specimens of Manhood: Schoolboy Literature and the Creation of a Colonial Chivalric Code." In *Imperialism and Juvenile Literature*. Jeffrey Richards, ed. Manchester, England, and New York: Manchester University Press, 1989; 173–194.

Murrell, Peter S.J. *The Imperial Idea in Children's Literature, 1840–1902*. Ph.D. diss., University of Wales, 1975.

Osa, Osayimwense. *African Children's and Youth Literature*. New York: Twayne Publishers, 1995.

Preiswerk, Roy. "Ethnocentric Images in History Books and Their Effect on Racism." In *The Black American in Books for Children: Readings on Racism*. 2d ed. Ed. Donnarae MacCann and Gloria Woodard. Metuchen, N.J.: Scarecrow Press, 1985; pp. 255–65.

_____. *The Slant of the Pen*. Geneva: World Council of Churches, 1980.

Randolph-Robinson, Brenda. "The Depiction of South Africa in Children's Literature." *Interracial Books for Children Bulletin* 15: 7 & 8 (1984): 14–22.

_____. "The Depiction of South Africa in U.S. Textbooks." *Interracial Books for Children Bulletin* 15: 7 & 8 (1984): 3–13.

Richards, Jeffrey. *Imperialism and Juvenile Literature*. Manchester, England, and New York: Manchester University Press, 1989.

Schmidt, Nancy J. *Children's Fiction About Africa in English*. Owerri, Nigeria and New York: Conch Magazine, 1981.

_____. *Children's Books on Africa and Their Authors*. New York: Africana Publishing Co., 1975.

_____. *Supplement to Children's Books on Africa and Their Authors*. New York: Africana Publishing Co., 1979.

Spidle, Jake W. "Victorian Juvenilia and the Image of the Black African." *Journal of Popular Culture* 9:1 (Summer 1975): 51–64.

Stones, Rosemary. "Multicultural Books in Britain: A Year of Contradictions." *Interracial Books for Children Bulletin* 8:1 (1977): 8–10.

Thornton, A.P. "G.A. Henty's British Empire." *Fortnightly Review* 175.6 (Jan.-June 1954): 97–101.

Other Books of Interest

Broderick, Dorothy. *Images of the Black in Children's Fiction*. New York: R.R. Bowker, 1973.

Coles, Robert. *The Political Life of Children*. Boston and New York: Atlantic Monthly Press, 1986.

Cooley, John R. *Savages and Naturals: Black Portraits by White Writers in Modern American Literature*. Cranbury, N.J.: University of Delaware Press, 1982.

Dummet, Ann. *A Portrait of English Racism*. Middlesex and Baltimore: Penguin Books, 1973.

Fredrickson, George M. *The Black Image in the White Mind: The Debate on Afro-American Character and Destiny, 1817–1914*. New York: Harper & Row, 1971. Reprint, Middletown, Conn.: Wesleyan University Press, 1987.

Gossett, Thomas. *Race: The History of an Idea in America*. Dallas: Southern Methodist University Press, 1963.

Henry, Zig Layton. *The Politics of Race in Britain*. London: Allen and Unwin, 1984.

MacCann, Donnarae, and Gloria Woodard, eds. *The Black American in Books for Children: Readings on Racism*. 2d ed. Metuchen, N.J.: Scarecrow Press, 1985.

MacCann, Donnarae. *The White Supremacy Myth in Juvenile Books about Blacks, 1830–1900*. Ph.D. diss., University of Iowa, 1988.

Nayareth, Peter. *The Third World Writer: His Social Responsibility*. Nairobi: Kenya Literature Bureau, 1978.

Rockwell, Joan. *Fact in Fiction: The Use of Literature in the Systematic Study of Society*. London: Routledge & Kegan Paul, 1974.

Small, Stephen. *Racialized Barriers: The Black Experience in the United States and England in the 1980s*. London and New York: Routledge, 1994.

Index